D0529613

Twayne's English Authors Series

Sylvia E. Bowman, *Editor*

INDIANA UNIVERSITY

Wilfred Owen

(TEAS) 86

Wilfred Owen

By GERTRUDE M. WHITE

Oakland University

Twayne Publishers, Inc.　　::　　New York

To F. F. M.
Who loved, and taught me to love, poetry.

Preface

THIS brief study of Wilfred Owen attempts to accomplish several aims. The first of these is to show Owen's growth as a poet, the forces that brought him to poetic maturity, and his attainment of an individual style. The book opens with a biographical account describing Owen's struggle to free himself from the intellectual and emotional limitations of his upbringing. Gradually, over a period of years, he came to reject his youthful world of fantasy and romance in favor of reality, and to replace the religious orthodoxy of his boyhood with a humanistic creed which he summed up in the phrase "greater love."

The first two-thirds of the book is devoted closely and specifically to a study of Owen and his poetry. In order to illustrate the nature and importance of the change which came over his poetry, Chapter 2 focuses on the dream world of Owen's early verse and discusses its relation to the whole Romantic tradition. Chapter 3 deals with the later, great poems of war; it describes the qualities, themes, and techniques of his mature poetry. Chapter 4 discusses Owen's poetic craftsmanship and prosodic innovations in more detail and analyzes the ways in which his great poems obtain their particular effects.

The growth of Wilfred Owen's reputation after his death furnishes a striking instance of the power of genuine poetry to survive, penetrate, influence, and grow in importance from the most unpromising beginnings. Chapter 5 surveys the slow but steady process by which Owen's poetry made its way into critical and popular esteem and points out contemporary evidence of the high position it has attained. Finally, Chapter 6 discusses certain critical questions raised by Owen's verse and by war poetry in general and compares him briefly with his fellow war poets in an effort to reach some conclusion as to the permanence of his stature and attainments.

Chronology is neither a safe nor a possible guide to the poems of Wilfred Owen. The state in which Owen's manuscripts were left at his early death makes it impossible to date many of them with certainty. In any case, the proper distinction is not between poems which are early or late chronologically but between those which are in his earlier or in his later, mature style. To the end of his life, when writing on subjects other than war, Owen was apt to revert to the diction, tone, and attitudes characteristic of his juvenile verses. The second chapter, "Weald of Youth," therefore, though it is chiefly a discussion of his youthful verse, includes such late poems as "Song of Songs," "Training," "The Roads Also," and "The Kind Ghosts." The justification for this will, I trust, be apparent in the text itself. On the other hand, all of Owen's great poems belong to the last year and a half of his life, and most—though not all—are war poems. These I have discussed in Chapters 3 and 4.

The reader who wishes more information about the dating of Owen's poems and about the problems of establishing a correct text will find these matters fully dealt with in D. S. R. Welland's book *Wilfred Owen: A Critical Study* (London, 1960). *The Collected Poems of Wilfred Owen*, edited by C. Day Lewis (London, 1963), contains a certain amount of information concerning the successive drafts of some of the poems, and Mr. Lewis' comments on some of the changes.

There have been many reviews and brief notices of Owen's work, but very few studies are of any length or importance. In the bibliography I have included all the studies I found of any real interest and have attempted to distinguish between the more and the less valuable, and to indicate those to which I am much indebted. The reader who wishes fuller details is referred to the bibliography of Owen cited in my own bibliography.

It is a pleasure to acknowledge, with a very lively sense of gratitude, the hospitality, interest, and help of Mr. Harold Owen, the poet's brother. To my husband, William White, I am indebted for his invaluable bibliographical aid, and for the patience with which he has lived with me and with Owen during the writing of this book. I should like to express my gratitude also to Patricia Hall, Adelaide Licklider, Gracia Ludvigh, and Marian Wilson.

GERTRUDE M. WHITE

Oakland University

Acknowledgments

Grateful acknowledgment of permission to quote is made to the following:

From THE COLLECTED POEMS of Wilfred Owen, edited by C. Day Lewis. Copyright @ Chatto & Windus, Ltd., 1963. Reprinted by permission of New Directions Publishing Corporation. For the use of excerpts from the poems and letters of Wilfred Owen, excerpts from Edmund Blunden's Memoir prefixed to that edition, and an excerpt from a letter by Mrs. Gray included in the Memoir. Also for Canadian and United Kingdom distribution rights.

The Oxford University Press for material from *Journey From Obscurity Wilfred Owen 1893–1918*, Volumes 1, 2, and 3 by Harold Owen, and for permission to reproduce a photograph of Owen in uniform.

Contents

Chronology

1893   March 18, Wilfred Edward Salter Owen born at Plas Wilmot, Oswestry, Shropshire.

1897   Owen family moved to Shrewsbury.

1898   Family moved to Birkenhead.

1900   April 30, Wilfred registered for entry into the Birkenhead Institute.

1907   Family returned to Shrewsbury. Wilfred began attending the Shrewsbury Technical School as a day boy.

1911   September, matriculated at London University, but owing to lack of money never attended classes. October, went to Dunsden, Oxfordshire, as lay assistant to the vicar, the Reverend Herbert Wigan.

1913   August, obtained post as a tutor in English at the Berlitz School of Languages, Bordeaux. September, left England to take up position.

1914   July, left Berlitz School; became tutor to two boys in a Catholic family in Bordeaux.

1915   September, returned to England. October, joined the Artists' Rifles.

1916   June 4, commissioned in Manchester Regiment. Late December, sailed to France on active service, attached to Lancashire Fusiliers.

1917   March 19, sent to 13th Casualty Clearing Station. Early April, returned to battalion. May 1 or 2, again sent to 13th Casualty Clearing Station, and from there to the 41st Stationary Hospital. June, went into No. 1 General Hospital, from which he was returned to England, arriving at the Welsh Hospital, Netley, about June 18. On June 26, was transferred to Craiglockhart War Hospital, Edinburgh. September 1, "Song of Songs," first of the four poems to be published in Owen's lifetime, appeared in the hospital magazine, *The Hydra*. November, discharged from Craig-lockhart and posted to Northern Cavalry Barracks, Scarborough.

1918 January 16, published "Miners" in *The Nation* (London). June 15, "Futility" and "Hospital Barge at Cérisy" published in *The Nation* (London). August 31 or September 1, returned to France on active service. October 1, awarded Military Cross for gallantry in action. November 4, killed by machine-gun fire, trying to get his company across the Sambre Canal.

CHAPTER 1

The Growth of a Poet's Mind

I *Introduction*

WILFRED Owen's short life was, until its final months, almost devoid of outer incident. Born into a cultivated but impoverished middle-class provincial family, he attended neither public school nor university. Delicate health, a studious temperament, and an early sense of vocation combined with poverty to cut him off from social life. He formed no close friendships. Until nearly the last year of his life he had little or no opportunity to meet other writers or men of letters. Indeed, his brief friendships with Laurent Tailhade, the French symbolist poet and pacifist, his elder by two generations, and with Siegfried Sassoon, his fellow poet and patient at Craiglockhart War Hospital, appear to have been his closest contacts with men who could understand and encourage his aspirations as a poet. He did not marry, nor did he, according to his brother's testimony, ever experience a close relationship with any woman. When he died in battle at the age of twenty-five, he was unknown as a poet to all but a handful of close acquaintances.

But a man's life is not measured by length of days or multiplicity of events. Owen's early death was an irreparable loss to English poetry; yet he had lived long enough to produce, in the face of seemingly insuperable odds, a number of poems of enduring value. Only four poems were published in his lifetime. At his death rough drafts on odd scraps of notepaper, the backs of menus or playbills, whatever paper he had happened to have with him in the hospital or the trenches, were found among his belongings. The devoted efforts of his mother and a few friends brought about publication, at first piecemeal in literary journals, then in 1920 in a small collection of twenty-three poems prepared from his manuscripts by Edith Sitwell and Siegfried Sassoon. Their extraordinary quality was at once recognized, and less than three years after his death Owen had already been hailed by such perceptive critics as John Middleton Murry as the best of the poets who had written during and of the First World War. Now, in the perspective of nearly fifty years, he is regarded by competent judges as not merely the best of the war poets but as perhaps the finest poet of his generation.

The key to this achievement lies in his earlier life as well as in the circumstances of war. It has often been stated that Owen was made a poet by the war. This seems plausible and gratifies our instinct for drama, but it is not true. Certainly there is a striking difference in tone and quality between the early verses and the late great poems of his maturity. And certainly he found his subject, as well as his own unique attitude toward it, in the experience of war. But he was already a poet long before he sailed to France on active service. He had recognized his vocation as early as the age of ten, and in the years that followed had concentrated all his powers on a long and arduous preparation for reaching this one goal.

Had Owen not dedicated himself from boyhood to a poet's calling, his introduction to war might well have overwhelmed rather than precipitated his poetry. The obscene ugliness and horror of trench warfare seared his senses and shook his nerves; but, whatever his sufferings as a man and a soldier, as a poet he stood firm. The Western Front could kill him, but it could not distort his vision nor impair his poetic self-control. His unwavering mastery of his terrible subject, his impersonal viewpoint, as well as his imaginative and moral force, distinguish Owen's best poems from those of his fellow war poets. Vision and control alike enlarge the significance of poems like "Strange Meeting," "The Show," "Futility," and "Anthem for Doomed Youth" to encompass not merely a particular historical but a universal human situation. How he attained that mastery is the story of Owen's life.

II Family and Early Life

Owen was born in 1893 at his mother's family home, Plas Wilmot at Oswestry in Shropshire. There was Welsh blood on both sides of the family; but, though he has been claimed by Welshmen as one of their own, he was English by immediate descent, by birth, by language, and by upbringing. Such cultural ties as he had outside England were with France, not Wales. He neither read nor spoke Welsh and knew no Welsh literature.

His father, a man of impatient and adventurous spirit who longed all his life to be a sailor, was condemned by circumstances to a dull and detested post, of considerable responsibility but very meager salary, with a railway. While still very young, he had sailed for India in hopes of finding better prospects for his future and that of the woman he hoped to marry. He had done well there, but after four years was forced by his own illness and misfortune in his intended wife's family to return to England to accept the best position he could find. For his family's sake he never thereafter dared to change, though he was deeply dissatisfied with his work, and longed with pathetic wistfulness for adventure and the sea.

After their marriage, he and his wife moved into her father's home and here, during Wilfred's first four years, the Owens were relatively well off and free from the strains and uncertainties of poverty. At the death of Mrs. Owen's father, however, it was discovered that he had for some time been living on his capital. "Never again," writes Harold Owen, the poet's younger brother, "to the end of their lives were they or their children once again to have any feeling of real security."[1] Plas Wilmot was sold, and the family moved first to a small, shabby house in the market town of Shrewsbury and not long after to an even smaller house in Birkenhead where Wilfred spent his boyhood.

These impoverished and somewhat embittered family circumstances were of decisive importance in Owen's life. Poverty meant far more than discomfort and deprivation in daily living. The parents were unable to provide for their children, even for the cherished and studious eldest son, the school and university education necessary for entrance into a profession or any position holding hopes of prosperity and advancement. Without the means to secure for their sons even a meager start in life, they could only hope that their boys might find, at an early age, humdrum but relatively safe jobs. The strains of their immediate life, augmented by anxiety for the future, affected their own relationship and their attitudes toward their children.

Wilfred, the eldest of four children, three boys and a girl, remained his mother's favorite; and his relationship with her was the closest one in his brief life. Harold Owen has described in the three volumes of his memoirs his mother's temperament and her attitudes within the family circle. In his pages, Mrs. Owen appears as a woman of exceptionally strong character and of deep, exceedingly narrow religious convictions. It is apparent that, consciously or unconsciously, she set out to compensate for the deprivations and frustrations of her life by binding her eldest son to her with unbreakable ties of emotional intimacy and dependence. She was his confidante and sole support in his ambition to become a poet, but her own ambition for him was that he might enter the Church. She seems to have been indifferent to the fact that her relationship with Wilfred meant the gradual but progressive alienation of the boy from his father.

Her husband was ardent, affectionate, and open by nature, but impatient and inarticulate and, furthermore, deeply disappointed in his career. He was wholly unable to cope with the alliance of wife and son and with the rifts and tensions created within the family. He bore the situation with dignity though not without pain, finding some solace himself in the companionship of his more active and robust younger son, Harold. It is pleasant to record that, years later, when Wilfred was teaching in Bordeaux, father and son discovered to their mutual surprise the pleasure each could take in the other's company outside the family circle. Meanwhile, however, the boy's father was to him a Philistine who neither understood nor valued his aspirations.

These family relationships are important, not for their own sake, but for the light they throw on Owen's development as a man and poet. In particular, his mother's character and her concentration on him profoundly affected his personal and poetic growth, though in ways she could neither have intended nor understood. The strength of his tie with her goes far to explain his failure to develop relationships with other women, and to account for the fact that so sensuous and ardent a young man shows in his life and in his poetry so little interest in sexual love. Mrs. Owen's influence has a bearing as well on other matters which are not, perhaps, so immediately obvious. It helps to explain Owen's rejection of orthodox Christianity either as profession or as emotional commitment. And—of more significance to his achievement as a poet—it accounts for one of the most striking characteristics of his best poetry: his calm, unflinching, almost terrifying honesty; his determination to confront reality without evasion; his steadfast refusal to avert his eyes from what he saw or his inner gaze from what he felt to be the truth. Owen's progress toward maturity, in fact, personal and poetic, was one of slow growth and weaning away from attitudes and limitations imposed on him by his upbringing.

In his early years, his mother's influence must have appeared to be all even she could desire. It was during a long holiday alone with her when he was only ten years of age that the boy felt stir within him the first awareness of his future calling:

> Where first I felt my boyhood fill
> With uncontainable movements; there was born
> My poethood.[2]

Though there is no evidence that he began to compose verse thus early, it is apparent that a sense of vocation had been awakened. "It was in Broxton," says his brother, "secure in the safety and understanding love that my mother wrapped about him . . . that the poetry in Wilfred . . . began to bud, and not on the battlefields of France." [3] Thus early, he was irretrievably dedicated to letters and, above all, to poetry.

Mrs. Owen's preoccupation with religion—that of the Established Church, but with its narrowest and most evangelical version—permeated her own life and strongly affected the atmosphere of her home. A rigid and puritanical piety was perhaps her most salient trait, and she cultivated the clergy and all the more superficial aspects of religion. It was inevitable that so attached a son should respond to this dominant concern; however, the manner of his boyhood response was curious and, to a student of Owen's poetry, suggestive. Harold Owen's autobiography records how, for a time, Wilfred delighted in playing the role of priest, dressing up in vestments made for him by his mother—including a bishop's miter—arranging and decorating the family living room with an improvised altar, candlesticks and flowers, and conducting a complete evening service even to the extent of preaching a short sermon. This phase seems not to have lasted very long, and it is evident that the boy's motive was theatrical rather than religious. His performance was not so much an act of faith and worship as one of self-dramatization accompanied by sensuous and emotional satisfaction. It was an incipient poet, rather than a priest, who impressed his younger brothers and sister on these family Sunday evenings.

In addition to her rather unimaginative piety, Mrs. Owen mani-
fested an extraordinary capacity for shutting her eyes and her
mind to unpleasant facts. This attitude, of course, derived not
only from temperament but at least partially from the Calvinistic
faith in which she had been reared. In her view, whatever was,
was right, was the will of God, and must be accepted and sub-
mitted to "with meek heart and due reverence" rather than ques-
tioned or opposed. Harold Owen tells how, in practice, this meant
that his mother resolutely refused to admit the existence of ugly
truths and "was content with the make-believe that they really
were non-existent. For her what was not nice must never in any
way be acknowledged." [4] In Harold's case, this attitude meant
that she saw him off to sea at the age of fifteen with a bland
disregard for the very real dangers, physical and moral, to which
he was exposed. The effects of her attitude were different and
more complicated on Wilfred, and they were not immediately apparent. They are clearly to be traced, however, in his later rejection both of the Church and of "Poetry."

Owen's rejection of "Poetry" in the manifesto he wrote toward
the end of his life as a preface to his projected volume of war
poems ("Above all, I am not concerned with Poetry") is well
known and has occasioned much discussion as to his exact meaning. More knowledge of his early life and of such episodes as
"Wilfred's Church," as his family called it, makes perfectly clear
what he meant and why he rejected not only "Poetry" but "religion" as well. He had early fallen in love with Keats, with whom
he strongly identified and whose influence is marked in his juvenile poetry. Hardly less marked is the influence of many other
nineteenth-century poets: Shelley, Tennyson, Swinburne, Wilde
and the poets of the 1890's, and to a lesser extent Wordsworth and
Matthew Arnold. Owen had, in fact, been nourished on popular
nineteenth-century Romantic poetry; and it is natural enough that
he should have fallen under the spell of what was most sensuous
as well as most grandiose, self-conscious and posturing, and
vaguely sentimental in that intoxicating mixture. "Poetry," then,
must early have meant to him—as we shall see in greater detail in
Chapter 2—beauty of word and cadence, titillation of the senses,
a rather vaporous and sentimental "uplift," a highly subjective
dalliance with a world of brightly colored fantasy, a chance to

dream and to dramatize, to test his own identity and to experiment with many attitudes and many roles.

"Wilfred's Church" tells us that in early life religion filled much the same place in his imagination as did poetry. Like most poets, Owen had little gift for abstract thought; his mind moved naturally in terms of image and symbol. He was attracted in boyhood by the drama, by the beauty and the mystery of ritual and sacrament, and by the opportunity it afforded him of "trying on" a part. He remained throughout his life responsive to the "beauty of holiness" as exemplified in the life and character of Christ, and in his later poetry he continued to draw heavily on Christian imagery and symbolism. Yet, as a young man ostensibly preparing for the Church, he revealed an impatience with theology that disconcerted the clergyman who was his tutor; and later still he rejected the Church and organized official Christianity as a guide to belief or the conduct of life. His dismissal of the Church was occasioned by his discovery that "religion," as he had been taught to understand it, had no connection with the reality he observed. For the same reason, when a little later he had come to his own poetic maturity, he rejected "Poetry."

In these early years, however, poetry and religion as he then knew them were absorbing his mind and virtually all his energies. But there is no question about which was his ruling passion: he was determined, his brother tells us, "that literature and the other arts should take precedence over all else in his life." [5] Convinced that scholarship alone could unlock the power within him, he turned to books with passionate intensity, shunning sports and play and taking as little part even in family activities as he could manage. This application, abetted by his mother, was the more baffling to his father in that he appeared to have no specific purpose nor to be preparing for any career. And his mother, though she encouraged his studies and furnished unwavering emotional support, had no real understanding either of literature or of his ambitions. Owen's life from boyhood until his early twenties was one of intense and solitary pursuit of a goal which no one near him could comprehend—and which he himself did not always see with clear and steady hope. His brother's account makes abundantly evident with what demons he wrestled: his passionate dedication to poetry and to achievement as a poet; his burning desire for learning and a wider life at a university as a means to his goal; his bitter knowledge that poverty barred his way; his morbid self-doubts and self-dissatisfaction; the sense of isolation which his mother's love could soothe but not banish; and, not least of all, his early and haunting conviction, all too accurately borne out, of premature death.

These years of intense inner strivings, painful and frustrating as they must have been, go far to explain the steely control and courage with which, as a poet, he confronted the worst that war could show him. The quiet, rather delicate, studious boy in the obscure provincial town was accustomed to battle before he heard the guns of the Somme. The battle was not merely to find a way out of the frustrations and limitations of his material circumstances, for even more important became his struggle to free himself from the limitations which his mother's vision had imposed on him and to see and assess for himself the meaning and the values of life.

By the time Wilfred had reached the middle teens, the question of his future had begun to cause his father great concern. He was a promising student at the Shrewsbury Technical School, absorbed in his books, but apparently without thought of what he should do for a living. According to Harold, Mr. Owen, anxious though not unsympathetic, "could not see how in our circumstances literature, much less poetry, could possibly make a living for Wilfred. He [Mr. Owen] found it difficult to share my mother's utterly unfounded and rather uncalculated optimistic view that everything would turn out all right somehow, and that if it didn't then it was further proof of God's will for all of us." [6] As we have noted, Mrs. Owen herself was secretly cherishing a hope that her favorite son would be able to enter the Church; and Wilfred was willing to entertain this possibility, not from a strong sense of vocation but because it would allow him to continue reading for a degree and hoping that some sort of opportunity would present itself. "No career in itself," says his brother, "made any definite appeal to him; for even at this age he was vaguely aware that all he really wanted was independence so that he could continue his reading and lever out of himself the creative poetic force which, uncertainly as yet, he knew to be in him. All that he could and did say was that he wanted independence from wage-earning for another five years. . . ." [7]

Upon graduation from the technical school, Wilfred sat for his matriculation at London University and passed moderately well. He had, however, no hope of actual entrance: the family simply could not afford it. In the midst of this uncertainty and anxiety Mrs. Owen, through her acquaintances among the clergy, learned of a vicar in Dunsden, Oxfordshire, who specialized in the preparation of young men for the Church. In return for tutoring, the students were expected to act as assistants to him in his parish work. Introductions were effected and the vicar, Mr. Herbert Wigan, having taken an immediate liking to Wilfred, offered him what amounted to an unofficial curacy. He was to receive room, board, and a token salary of five shillings a week in return for his help in the parish, and was to have tuition and time for reading and preparation. The vicar further promised to use what influence he could to obtain a scholarship for entrance to Oxford should the young man prove willing to enter the Church.

But Wilfred, already beset by grave doubts, showed unexpected firmness in refusing to commit himself; and, after a certain amount of hesitation and reluctance, Mr. Wigan agreed that he should have two years to make up his mind. The prospect, if not exhilarating, at least offered him independence of his family, a respite from wage-earning, and an opportunity for tutoring and reading. Perhaps more important, it offered also a chance to continue the writing of verses, which had by now begun to absorb him. He departed for Dunsden in October, 1911, at the age of eighteen.

III *Dunsden and France*

His mother's unaccustomed decision and energy had obtained for the young man this opportunity for continued study and the possibility of entrance into the Church. The effect of the fifteen months at Dunsden, however, was altogether contrary to her hopes and expectations. Owen's work as unofficial curate confirmed both his doubts about orthodox religious doctrine and his hesitations about his own vocation for the Church. His experiences among the poor of the parish developed in him insights and attitudes altogether alien to his mother's habit of mind, and of prime importance to his growth as a poet. Although he found his parish duties grindingly hard, he carried them out conscientiously. Mr. Wigan proved disappointing as a tutor—having himself been disappointed in his pupil's intentions—so that Wilfred was thrown back for his reading on his own resources. But his experiences in the course of his parish duties so affected him that they began the process of change which was to bring about his maturity as a man and a poet.

Owen was not at this time an altogether attractive figure. His preferred position within the family circle, his absorption in books and intense ambition to make himself a poet, the difficulties and frustrations of his circumstances, the impact on him of his mother's attitudes—all had combined to make him egocentric, intolerant, overcritical, and wholly unable to understand or to take a sympathetic interest in the feelings and troubles of others. His own inner world engrossed his attention and energies. His outlook was narrow and rigid, his values extremely limited, his experience of life so circumscribed as to be virtually nonexistent. But, away from home and brought into daily contact with a poverty and squalor far worse than that experienced by his own family, he began to emerge from himself and his dreams. His introspection and self-absorption were for the first time penetrated by the sufferings and the needs of others. Dunsden was the beginning of the compassion and the power of identification which was to characterize so strongly his later life and poetry. And this first impact on him of the realities of life brought about not only a change in his character but a revulsion from the religion which home and Church represented.

It seems clear that it was not intellectual doubts of the validity of Christian dogma that alone weaned Owen from the Church as a profession and from faith in orthodox institutional Christianity. These doubts he had entertained for some time, as his reluctance to commit himself wholeheartedly to preparation for the Church attests. Now his experiences at Dunsden revealed to him forcibly the utter lack of connection—as it seemed to him—between the doctrine and discipline of the Church and the real lives of ordinary people. In a letter to his brother Wilfred denounced the Established Church as a complete divergence from the teachings of Christ; but, at the same time, he counseled Harold to read the New Testament and perceive for himself "the true poetry in the Man and his life." [8] To his mother he wrote, "I have murdered my false creed. If a true one exists, I shall find it. If not, adieu to the still falser creeds that hold the hearts of nearly all my fellow men." [9]

Dunsden, then, reinforced his doctrinal doubts with concrete experience of the Church's failure to meet the most pressing material needs of real people. The Founder of Christianity had identified Himself with the poor and the suffering; the Established Church of England appeared to be indifferent to them. To Wilfred Owen, a great deal of what the Church preached and stood for began to seem not only shallow and meaningless but consciously insincere.

Nothing of what must have amounted to a quiet revolution in his heart and mind as yet showed in the verses he was writing. His poems at this time were still preoccupied with a dream world, with fantasies of love, of beauty, and of fame. His indignant scorn and protest against callousness and hypocrisy speak only in his letters. But the way was being prepared for his response to the bloodshed and horror of war; for the great poems of his poetic maturity, with their steadfast honesty of observation and emotion; for the profound and unsentimental compassion—the power of identification with the sufferings of others—which is his hallmark as a poet. Rejecting formal Christianity and all that "religion" had once connoted to him, as later he was to reject "Poetry" declaring that "The Poetry is in the pity," he began to turn instead to the "greater love" embodied in human suffering and sacrifice for others.

In the winter of 1913 Owen suffered a severe illness, probably owing not a little to his anxieties and dissatisfactions, and certainly something to the damp climate of Oxfordshire and his unheated bedroom at the vicarage. A real or imagined threat of consumption added to his perturbations. Illness combined with disillusion to resolve his long dilemma. With bitter disappointment he at last began to face the truth: his university hopes were impossible of fulfillment. He had come to a point where he realized that his immediate environment offered him no hope of wider opportunities, intellectual stimulation, or encouragement in his poetic ambitions and that he must seek elsewhere what he needed. For years he had been a student of French literature and the French language, feeling a peculiar and intuitive rapport with French culture. It was to France, therefore, that he turned. Answering an advertisement by the Berlitz School of Languages, he obtained a part-time post teaching English in its school in Bordeaux. In September, 1913, he left England to take up this position.

The effect of France was to confirm and consolidate the process which had began at Dunsden. It set him free to think, unhampered by the conventions and platitudes of home and Church. He continued to acquire perspective on himself, to emerge from his self-absorption and egocentrism, to rid himself of the overcritical intolerance and the overconfident reliance on his own judgment, untempered by experience, which his mother's example and influence had encouraged. His teaching could not have been stimulating—he left the Berlitz School in less than a year to become tutor to two boys in a Bordeaux family—but he had the good fortune to meet and strike up a friendship with M. Laurent Tailhade, a French symbolist poet, the first professional poet the young man had ever met. Though Tailhade had no direct influence on Owen's own poetry, his warm, sympathetic interest and encouragement must have meant a great deal to the lonely youngster. The elder man was also a pacifist, a fact which perhaps did have some effect on the development of Owen's attitude toward war.

Owen's first reaction, however, when war burst over Europe in the fateful summer of 1914, was not typical of either humanitarian or pacifist, but of the earlier self he was only painfully and slowly outgrowing. As earlier he had resented the noisy intrusions of his younger brothers in hours of study, he now resented the even noisier intrusion of war and the threat it presented to his poetry and all his literary ambitions. Far from feeling any patriotic ardor, he was determined only to preserve for himself the opportunity to continue his writing at all costs. He saw the war as only another barrier to the achievement of his ambitions. It seems not to have been until the spring of 1915 that he began to be troubled by doubts and perplexities.

When doubts did assail him, he revealed the self-control, the integrity, and the sense of responsibility which had been developing in him. He was resolved not to be swept away by excitement or the emotional satisfaction of taking the popular course, not to be driven by fears of being called coward, not to be coerced by outer pressures, but to make a reasoned and responsible decision. "I am determined to think for myself and act only when I know which road I must take," he wrote to his brother.[10] This resolution to preserve his own inner truth, to exert the control of mind and will over circumstances, and to accept the responsibility for his own actions speaks most eloquently in the great poems written in the last year of his life.

Owen returned to England in September, 1915. In October, doubts as to his best course of action apparently resolved, he joined the Artists' Rifles. Eight months later, on June 4, 1916, he was commissioned in the Manchester Regiment; and in late December he departed once more for France, this time on active service, attached to the Lancashire Fusiliers.

IV *War*

The war to which Owen was introduced at the very end of 1916 was far different from the one that had been entered into with such enthusiasm, optimism, and visions of glory as are hymned in the poems of Rupert Brooke and other lesser poets. "Now, God be thanked Who has matched us with His hour," exulted Brooke, so soon to die before he could learn the bitter realities of that hour. The great offensive of the Somme, the chief bid of British arms to win a decisive victory, had faded into a stalemate that saw the end of hopes for triumph or early peace. Its enormous losses— sixty thousand casualties on the first day of battle alone—had drained the army of strength and of easy confidence. There ensued the long-drawn-out agony of static trench warfare, surely the most dismal and devastating form of conflict which men have endured. It was this war of attrition and helpless misery that Owen knew and of which he wrote.

Accounts of World War I, in countless memoirs, poems, plays, and novels, have made familiar the main features of that conflict even to a generation not born till after World War II. Everywhere, there was the inescapable ugliness, physical misery, and horror. A blasted landscape, riddled with shellholes, dotted with the ruins of trees and houses, and littered with the shattered bodies of men and animals, presented a scene out of the *Inferno*. Day after day of rain turned the sticky clay to liquid mud, so deep in places that men were known to drown in it. Over everything hung the characteristic stench of the battlefields, compounded of the reek of latrines and the stink of long-unburied corpses. Filth, fatigue, and pain wearied the body; the constant spectacle of senseless violence and bestiality, waste and corruption, first revolted and then numbed the mind. The sight of death, in the vil-

est and most degrading forms that could assault the flesh, charred
the senses of soldiers; and the constant fear of it disordered their
nerves. The fortunate endured and lived; the unfortunate endured, suffered, and died; some went mad; others shot themselves, courting wounds that would send them home, or even to
the death from which they shrank. As for Owen,

They want to call No Man's Land "England" because we keep
supremacy there. It is like the eternal place of gnashing of teeth; the
Slough of Despond could be contained in one of its crater-holes; the
fires of Sodom and Gomorrah could not light a candle to it—to find
the way to Babylon the Fallen. It is pock-marked like a body of foulest
disease, and its odour is the breath of cancer. I have not seen any
dead. I have done worse. In the dank air I have *perceived* it, and in
the darkness, *felt*. . . . No Man's Land under snow is like the face
of the moon, chaotic, crater-ridden, uninhabitable, awful, the abode
of madness.[11]

Another letter from this period of his first service in the trenches
reveals in one of its phrases how swiftly his experiences were al-
tering his early views: "Hideous landscapes, vile noises, foul language, and nothing but foul, even from one's own mouth (for all
are devil-ridden)—everything unnatural, broken, blasted; the dis-
tortion of the dead, whose unburiable bodies sit outside the dug-
outs all day, all night, the most execrable sights on earth. In poetry we call them the most glorious." [12] "In poetry we call them the
most glorious!" Poets from Horace to Sir Henry Newbolt had
written of honor and glory, of flags and cavalry charges, of
"might, majesty, dominion, and power," and had called death in
battle sweet. So, in the Preface written shortly before his own
death in battle, Wilfred Owen declared that English poetry was
not yet fit to speak of heroes; he disclaimed glory and honor; and
he declared that, "My subject is War, and the pity of War. The
Poetry is in the pity."

To the horrors of actual war, disillusionment was added. Men
began to suspect the actions and the motives of their own government. They were prepared to encounter the valor and stubborn-
ness of the enemy; they were resigned to bureaucratic muddle
and the arrogance and incompetence of staff officers; but the
thought of actual betrayal by politicians for sordid ends was intolerable. The official attitude of the Church in support of the war

also disillusioned men who were doing the actual fighting: to them, the German front-line soldier was a fellow sufferer in this hellish and senseless conflict, while from the pulpits of Christian churches the servants of Christ preached hatred of "the Boche" and, ignoring physical and political realities, continued to use such terms as "crusade" and "righteous war." Many soldiers felt in an inarticulate way what Owen was to voice in his poetry—that they, rough and foul-mouthed as they were, knew more of true religion than the preachers and chaplains who prattled such phrases and offered to their most urgent needs only comfortless platitudes. In their suffering, comradeship, and sacrifice, they instinctively felt, they were far closer to Christ than those who pretended to speak for Him.

Going home on leave, for many, was the worst disillusionment of all. With a sense of bitter isolation they perceived the great gulf between fighting man and civilian. In the trenches, they were at least knit together in a comradeship and love passing the love of women. Back in England, they encountered ignorance, callous indifference, or shrill hatred of an enemy whom they did not hate. Only the war itself was worthy of their hatred. Lies in the press, sentimental or calculating; propaganda spewing from government offices; the porcine Leeds and Bradford millionaire war profiteers; the hateful attitudes and actions of noncombatants; the whole tone of civilian life—all combined to embitter and disenchant men far less sensitive than poets.

Outwardly, Owen was a typical young infantry officer, indistinguishable from thousands of others. Having decided to participate, he deliberately cultivated outward conformity, not for advantage but in the conviction that his inward power would thus be enhanced. Harold Owen tells of the apparent change that came over him, transforming him from a quiet, untidy, delicate-appearing boy, out of place and uncomfortable in his army camp surroundings, to a smart, self-assured officer at ease with himself and commanding the respect of his men. "I was impressed enormously by an air which hung about him of tremendous soldierly competence. . . . Altogether his air of assurance and complete mastery of himself as a fighting officer was impressive." [13] That this change was the result of a deliberate effort at self-mastery Wilfred's own words to his brother confirm: "You know, Harold, if I have got to be a soldier, I must be a good one, anything else is unthinkable. I cannot alter myself inside nor yet conform but at least without any self-questioning I can change outside, if that is what is wanted . . . outwardly I will conform . . . my inward force will be the greater for it." [14] Inwardly, he preserved and strengthened his power of intellectual and critical detachment, resolved to maintain at all costs the integrity of his own mind and spirit.

The official account of Owen's war service is still buried in File No. 38/0/1118, at the War Records Centre in Droitwich. Until very recently, the fullest report of it was Edmund Blunden's Memoir first affixed to the 1931 edition of Owen's poems and reprinted in C. Day Lewis' 1963 volume, *The Collected Poems of Wilfred Owen*. In the autumn of 1967, however, appeared the long-awaited *Collected Letters* edited by the poet's brother, Harold Owen, and John Bell, and published by the Oxford University Press. Owen's life during these years can now be followed almost from day to day through the hundreds of letters—most of them written to his mother—contained in this volume.

In the early winter of 1917 Owen took part in some of the hardest fighting the Manchester Regiment had experienced, in the coldest weather of the war. Toward the middle of March he suffered a concussion from a fall into a cellar and was invalided out of the line for a few days, but rejoined his battalion before the end of the month. April was a cruel month of midnight patrols, sharp attacks, shelling which occasioned him several narrow escapes, and days of unrelieved stand-to: "For twelve days I did not wash my face, nor take off my boots, nor sleep a deep sleep. For twelve days we lay in holes, where at any moment a shell might put us out." [15] It was during this period that he was blown bodily from his hole in a railway embankment by a shell that landed only six feet away, and found on recovery that a brother officer had been buried alive just across from him: ". . . no relief will ever relieve him, nor will his Rest be a 9-days-Rest." [16]

On May 2, 1917, Owen was in the 13th Casualty Clearing Station, the victim of a condition then labeled "neurasthenia." "I did not go sick or anything," he wrote to his mother, "but he [the doctor] is nervous about my nerves . . . I still of course suffer from the headaches traceable to my concussion. . . . Do not for a moment suppose I have had a 'breakdown'! I am simply avoiding one." [17] His state was, however, sufficiently serious for him to be

sent, by slow stages, to the Craiglockhart War Hospital at Ed
burgh, a place of treatment for officers suffering from disordered
nerves—"shell shock," as it was called. Here Owen was to remain
until November.

V *Craiglockhart*

His stay at Craiglockhart was of prime importance to him as a
poet. It provided rest and time for reflection, time to muse on the
meaning of his war experiences, to work on his poetry, and even
to publish. "Song of Songs," his first poem to appear in print, was
published in *The Hydra,* the hospital magazine which Owen was
then editing. Most important of all, it brought him into close companionship with another poet, Siegfried Sassoon, whose friendship
was not only significant to him personally during the remaining
year of his life, but largely instrumental in establishing his reputation after his death.

Sassoon, Owen's senior by six years, had already published several volumes of poetry, the latest of which, *The Old Huntsman,*
Owen had recently read and admired.[18] Sassoon's military history
as well was guaranteed to appeal to the younger man. He had
enlisted early in the war and had served at the front with a reck-
less courage that earned him the nickname "Mad Jack." While still
in the trenches he had composed antiwar poems; and a leave in
England which brought him in contact with the pacifist group
centering on Lady Ottoline Morrell had strengthened his growing
conviction that the war was being unnecessarily and deliberately
prolonged by "the gang" in power. He had thrown his Military
Cross into the River Mersey and had written a letter to his commanding officer refusing to participate further in the senseless
slaughter. The result of this, instead of the expected court-martial,
was his consignment to Craiglockhart as a sufferer from "shell
shock."

Sassoon's influence on Owen has so often been mentioned that
it should be made clear in what that influence consisted. On
Owen's poetry, Sassoon had little direct influence, a fact to which
he himself testifies in his autobiography, *Siegfried's Journey,
1916–1920.* The two men were dissimilar in temperament and in
talent, and Sassoon's vein of savage satire was not one that Owen
could profit by imitating. Irony and indignation, present though
they undoubtedly are in Owen's great poems, are held in check by

a far larger, much less personal viewpoint, a tone and manner
deeper, graver, more elegiac. His genius, in fact, is not only different from Sassoon's but of a higher order altogether, and his poetic
development had already proceeded too far by the time the two
men met for him to be deflected from his own course by another's
example. In fact, it seems, surprisingly enough, that the reverse is
true. By Sassoon's own testimony in *Siegfried's Journey*, his
verse was coming to be influenced by the impersonal attitude
which Owen was perfecting. "Unconsciously," Sassoon tells us, "I
was getting nearer to Wilfred Owen's method of approach." [19]

What Sassoon did provide was understanding and encouragement, the stimulus and companionship of a brother poet close to
Owen's own age, and the inestimable benefit of commentary at
once sympathetic and objective on work already done. It is hard
to exaggerate how much the sense of his friendship and support
must have meant to the lonely and nerve-strained young man.
Tailhade had been his senior by forty-odd years, and a French-
man at that; Sassoon was an English poet and a contemporary.
When Owen wrote so proudly and pathetically to his mother on
New Year's Eve, 1917, "I am held peer by the Georgians; I am a
poet's poet. I am started. The tugs have left me; I feel the great
swelling of the open sea taking my galleon," [20] it was no doubt
chiefly of Sassoon that he was thinking. "Fame is the recognition
of one's peers," he told her in a later letter. "I have already more
than their recognition." [21] This recognition was the result of another service Sassoon rendered the young poet, introducing him
for the first time to a circle of authors and men of letters. Among
them were Osbert Sitwell, young Guards officer, poet, and leader
of a literary coterie in rebellion against the more traditional Georgians; Robert Ross, who had been the staunch friend and sup-
porter of Oscar Wilde; and H. G. Wells and Arnold Bennett, both
already established as among the leading novelists of the time.

Nevertheless, despite the capacity for reverence and hero worship which caused Owen sometimes to express himself in his letters in overemotional terms, the relationship between him and
Sassoon was closer to that of equals than has generally been recognized. A letter from Owen to Sassoon is almost rhapsodic in its
expression of admiration and indebtedness: "Know that since mid-
September, when you still regarded me as a tiresome little
knocker on your door, I held you as Keats + Christ + Elijah +

my Colonel + my father-confessor + Amenophis IV in profile.
What's that mathematically? . . . And you have fixed my life—
however short." He continues, however, with what amounts to a
declaration of poetic independence: "I spun round you a satellite
for a month, but I shall swing out soon, a dark star in the orbit
where you will blaze." [22]

To the younger man, Sassoon might be, by virtue of poetry and
protest alike, a sort of avatar; but no amount of reverence, it is
clear, could sway him from his sense of what his own course must
be. And it is also clear that Sassoon, though admitting that not
until after Owen's death did he fully recognize his quality as a
poet, held his friend in both affection and esteem. His autobiography records the sense of sore and angry loss with which the news
of Owen's death afflicted him, and his labors in behalf of early
publication of Owen's poetry are sufficient witness to his regard
for the man as well as the poet.

To Owen's sojourn at Craiglockhart and the months of light
duty at Scarborough that followed, we owe most of his best
poems. This period witnessed an amazing burst of creative power,
an *annus mirabilis* indeed in which he was producing poem after
poem in an intensity of concentration and purpose. The forces
that had been slowly shaping him had brought him to poetic po-
tency and resolution, and he had fashioned for himself a voice of
such authentic and individual tone that no faintest echo of his
great predecessors remains. The poems of this period sound the
unmistakable note of a unique personality and point of view; and,
as Coleridge remarked of certain lines by Wordsworth, we should
recognize them if we met them running wild in the deserts of
Arabia.

The moral and emotional pressure under which he now wrote
was greater than ever before. All self-doubts and hesitations about
the part he had to play had been swept away by his experiences of
actual war. He had dreamed since boyhood of achievement and
fame as a poet, but he now knew to what end his dreams and
struggles had been directed. He would tell the truth about war, in
the hope that "he might in some minute way lessen the bitter and
unholy suffering and perhaps by some action of his strike at the
conscience of England and civilization." [23] His Preface to the collection of poems he planned and the tentative table of contents
giving the titles of poems he chose for the volume, together with

his motive for including them, show how his thoughts were running. The Preface in its entirety reads:

This book is not about heroes. English poetry is not yet fit to speak of them.

Nor is it about deeds, or lands, nor anything about glory, honour, might, majesty, dominion, or power, except War.

Above all I am not concerned with Poetry.

My subject is War, and the pity of War.

The Poetry is in the pity.

Yet these elegies are to this generation in no sense consolatory. They may be to the next. All a poet can do today is warn. That is why the true Poets must be truthful.

(If I thought the letter of this book would last, I might have used proper names; but if the spirit of it survives—survives Prussia—my ambition and those names will have achieved themselves fresher fields than Flanders. . . .)[24]

The title page is even more revealing. Some of his "Motives," accompanied by the title of the poem which was to illustrate them are: "How the future will forget the dead in war" ("Miners"); "The unnaturalness of weapons" ("Arms and the Boy"); "Madness" ("The Chances" and "Aliens"); "Heroic Lies" ("Letter"); "Inhumanity of War" ("Inspection" and "The Last Word"—a title later changed to "The Last Laugh"); "Indifference at Home"— ("Dulce et Decorum" and "Dead Beat"); "Willingness of old to sacrifice young" ("Parable"); "The insupportability of war" ("S.I.W."—a military abbreviation meaning "self-inflicted wound"); "Mentality of Troops + Vastness of Losses, with reflections on Civilians" ("Draft"); "Horrible beastliness of war" ("The Show"); "Grief" (several titles were included in this category, "Anthem for Doomed Youth" and "Futility" among them); "Foolishness of War" ("Strange Meeting").[25] It is evident that he intended to make in his poetry a systematic survey of the entire panorama of modern war, exposing its true nature and its effects on soldier, civilian, and society at large. His poems were to be not merely individual lyric, narrative, or descriptive pieces; each was to be part of a larger picture revealing the face of war.

Owen's return to the front after more than a year in England was the inescapable result of the process that had brought him to personal and poetic maturity. This process, at first slow and secret, worked in him while he toiled at his books in Shrewsbury, quickened during his parish work at Dunsden, continued at Bordeaux, and was brought to full fruition by the shock of war. The self-absorption and egocentrism of his youth had been replaced by an empathy and power of identification with suffering that had burned away selfhood. "His sensitiveness, his sympathy were so acute, so profound, that direct personal experience and individual development can hardly be said to have existed for him. He could only suffer, or rejoice, vicariously," wrote a friend of Craiglockhart days.[26] He had earlier acknowledged inescapable responsibility for himself; then for the soldiers serving and suffering with him; and finally for England and all mankind. His first tour of active duty had left him with the profound conviction that war was utterly and absolutely evil:

Already I have comprehended a light which never will filter into the dogma of any national church: namely, that one of Christ's essential commands was: Passivity at any price! Suffer dishonour and disgrace, but never resort to arms. Be bullied, be outraged, be killed; but do not kill. It may be a chimerical and an ignominious principle, but there it is. It can only be ignored; and I think pulpit professionals are ignoring it very skilfully and successfully indeed. . . . And am I not myself a conscientious objector with a very seared conscience? . . . Christ is literally in "no man's land." There men often hear His voice: Greater love hath no man than this, that a man lay down his life for a friend. Is it spoken in English only and French? I do not believe so. Thus you see how pure Christianity will not fit in with pure patriotism.[27]

Christ, to Owen, by this time had come to mean human love, suffering, and sacrifice—the "greater love" which he celebrated in his poetry; and Christ was rejected alike by Church and State. Like Edith Cavell, Owen would have said, "Patriotism is not enough." Nor was the religion of his upbringing enough. What counted was the love and solidarity of suffering men, all of them Christs in what they endured for others.

In a letter written to Osbert Sitwell in July, 1918, when Owen was training troops in England, he embodies this vision in an explicit and vivid figure: "For 14 hours yesterday I was at work—teaching Christ to lift his cross by numbers, and how to adjust his crown; and not to imagine he thirst till after the last halt. I attended his Supper to see that there were not complaints; and inspected his feet that they should be worthy of the nails. I see to it that he is dumb, and stands at attention before his accusers. With a piece of silver I buy him every day, and with maps I make him familiar with the topography of Golgotha." [28]

And so, acknowledging his own share in the guilt of the world, he felt that he must return to the trenches the more strongly and surely to voice his protest. Poetry for him was no longer the satisfaction of a sense of beauty and romance, no longer the attaining of a personal ambition. It was a means of speaking for those who could not speak for themselves and, through his voice, of awakening perhaps the conscience of England and the world. To his mother he wrote from the front: "I came out in order to help these boys—directly by leading them as well as an officer can, indirectly by watching their sufferings that I may speak of them as well as a pleader can." [29] One of his last comments on his own poetry, in a letter to Sassoon, expresses his sense of identification with his men: "I don't want to write anything to which a soldier would say *No compris!*" [30] Not despite but because of his perception of the evil and agony of war, and his destined role as spokesman, he returned to take part again in the conflict and to die.

From Craiglockhart he had been sent for light duty to Scarborough and put in charge of the hotel where the officers of the 5th Reserve Battalion of the Manchester Regiment assembled for additional training before returning to the front. Here he remained until the late summer of 1918. At the end of August, refusing all efforts by some of his new friends in literary circles to find some post that would keep him in England, he re-embarked for France. He went in the certainty of death, as Harold Owen's report of a conversation during Wilfred's last home leave tells. He had always suffered from premonitions that his life would be cut short. His knowledge of conditions on the Western Front now confirmed him in this conviction.

The end was not long in coming. Owen was posted to his old battalion and was in action at once. He won the Military Cross for his gallantry during an attack that left only one other officer alive in the company. On November 4, exactly one week before the Armistice, he was helping the Engineers bridge the Sambre

Canal, which his company had to cross, when he was struck by machine-gun fire and killed.

For his grave at Ors, his mother chose his own words from a sonnet called "The End," which reads in full:

> After the blast of lightning from the east
> The flourish of loud clouds, the Chariot Throne;
> After the drums of time have rolled and ceased,
> And by the bronze west long retreat is blown,
>
> Shall Life renew these bodies? Of a truth
> All death will he annul, all tears assuage?—
> Or fill these void veins full again with youth,
> And wash, with an immortal water, Age?
>
> When I do ask white Age he saith not so:
> "My head hangs weighed with snow."
> And when I hearken to the Earth, she saith:
> "My fiery heart shrinks, aching. It is death.
> Mine ancient scars shall not be glorified,
> Nor my titanic tears, the seas, be dried."

On his gravestone, Mrs. Owen caused the words to be inscribed thus: "Of a truth/All death will He annul, all tears assuage."

Owen had originally written "God" in the fifth line of the sonnet, but had firmly struck it out and substituted "Life." He had replaced his original phrase "The righteous" with "these bodies." Edmund Blunden's edition of Owen's poems prints the capitalized word "He" in the sixth line: "All death will He annul, all tears assuage?—"; but as Day Lewis, the most recent editor of Owen's poems, points out in his edition, in which the word is printed without capitals, "Owen's emendations in the previous line indicate that he wished the Deity to be kept out of this poem." [31] The omission on the gravestone of the question mark at the end of the sixth line is Mrs. Owen's own emendation;[32] and, of course, it changes the entire meaning of the poem. Converting a question, to which the poet himself returns a negative, to a statement of affirmation and faith, the bereaved mother thus reverses her son's intention and imposes her own.

Pathos and irony! The mutilated quotation might stand as a symbol of their relationship. Owen had achieved his boyhood ambition of poethood by slowly and painfully freeing himself from the trammels cast about him by temperament and upbringing. In doing so, he had left his mother far behind and on a different path altogether. Perhaps it is as well that she could not allow herself to realize how far he had traveled from her since those early days at Broxton.

The distance that lay between Broxton and the Somme can be gauged only by those who acquaint themselves with Owen's early verses as well as with his great poems of war. Students of Owen's poetry cannot afford to ignore his juvenilia, as for the most part they have been ignored. Few of them are of real value as poems, but they show much that is important to an understanding of Owen's mature poetry and of the attitudes it expresses and embodies. They illustrate how congenial the whole Romantic tradition was to his youthful temperament, and with what effort he freed himself from its grip. They show also how attenuated and artificial that tradition had become. As one Georgian observed, poetry had to become brutal before it could once again be human. And not least important to a student of English poetry, these verses exhibit his early and continuing experiments with sound patterns, the sense of the musical value of words which is one of his principal gifts. It is, therefore, to the dream world of Owen's early verses that we must first turn.

"Weald of Youth": The Early Poetry

> I broider the world upon a loom,
> I broider with dreams my tapestry;
> Here in a little lonely room
> I am master of earth and sea,
> And the planets come to me.
>
> I broider my life into the frame,
> I broider my love, thread upon thread;
> The world goes by with its glory and shame,
> Crowns are bartered and blood is shed;
> I sit and broider my dreams instead.
>
> And the only world is the world of my dreams,
> And my weaving the only happiness;
> For what is the world but what it seems?
> And who knows but that God, beyond our guess,
> Sits weaving worlds out of loneliness?

ARTHUR Symons, cultivated representative of the literary world of the 1890's, the friend of Oscar Wilde, Ernest Dowson, W. B. Yeats, and Lionel Johnson, a member of the Rhymers' Club, a poet and esthete, thus describes his own verses. In so doing, he also describes Wilfred Owen's early poems, which are indeed woven out of dreams of love, of beauty, of fame. Occasionally more sinister phantasms rise from darker depths, and the dreams come perilously close to nightmare. But no voice intrudes from the outer world, and the poet dreams on. "In dreams begins responsibility," said the older Yeats, but the young Owen as yet knew no responsibilities. His dream world was to him more intensely real and meaningful than the world his body inhabited.

Owen's dream world, however, was not a private domain. Bards had held it in fealty to Apollo since Homer's time. More especially was it the preserve of the nineteenth century, the imaginative world of the great Romantic poets. By Owen's time, the morning freshness of the early century had vanished; the dreams had become feverish and sickly. They had been tossed and troubled by the age's perplexities, and by strange currents flowing from France. No longer was Romanticism a vision of larger life but a refuge from modern pains and problems or a defiant challenge to the Philistines. It had lost touch with the springs of life and become artificial, repetitive, hollow, rhetorical, meaningless.

It is the artificiality, the "literary" quality of Owen's early verse, which most strikes the reader familiar with English poetry. The dreamer shares his imaginary world with so many other poets, bygone or contemporary, that all we hear is the echo of a multitude of voices. In that chorus, any individual note is drowned. These poems are subjective, but they are not really personal: they are self-absorbed but not private. Everywhere there is a luxuriance of egocentrism, a romantic self-dramatization, a playing with themes and attitudes in a self-conscious, theatrical manner that leaves no opportunity for the intrusion of reality. Nothing true to life, nothing sincere, is here save by a kind of accident. Now and again a tone of voice, a turn of phrase, an image, a hint of honest emotion give a glimpse of the poet Owen was to become.

I *Keats*

The influence of Keats is everywhere detectable in these early verses—but not the Keats of the letters and of the great odes; the poet whose later style exemplifies that "union of intensity and restraint" which his biographer so justly bids us admire;[1] the Keats who himself bade the too-prolix Shelley to "load every rift with ore." In Owen's poetry we meet the juvenile, more languid Keats whose luscious verses the tougher-minded Byron scorned. In verbal melody, in subject matter and mood, in diction and image, Owen's early poems again and again pay homage to the poet he reverenced and with whose aspirations and fate he identified.

As yet there is no evidence of the great power which Owen, as he matured, came to share with the mature Keats: the capacity for empathic identification with others, the emptying of self, that stamps the great poems of both men with a high disinterestedness, an impersonality that leaves no room for the obtrusion of personal feelings. Owen's war poetry was to illustrate this power in the highest degree, but that time was not yet come. Instead, he was absorbed in imitating the more readily copied characteristics of Keats: the familiar allusions to and figures drawn from Classical mythology; the conventional "poetic" diction, artificial and at times archaic; the delight in the senses; the rich and glowing colors and lush images, the soft prettiness; the verbal beauty of cadence and rhythm, of vowel and consonant. Here too are the familiar themes: the ideal of poetry as "a friend/To soothe the cares, and lift the thoughts of man" [2] and the thirst for glory, the poet's laurel crown. Here is the longing for the ideal and the immortal, so prominent throughout Keats's poetry; and Keats's recurrent treatment of dreaming and waking.

"On My Songs," a sonnet dated January 4, 1913, reads like a deliberate attempt at imitating Keats, just as in some of Keats's early verses he deliberately imitated his master Spenser. Owen's sonnet is hybrid in form, the poet perhaps not quite sure at what effect he is aiming. It preserves the rhyme scheme of the English sonnet until the final two lines, where Owen avoids ending on the precise and definite note afforded by the couplet; but it exhibits the break between octave and sestet characteristic of the Italian sonnet, sharply marked by a shift in subject. The theme is familiar: the power of poetry composed by men long dead to fill the mind and the imagination of living men, a theme frequently dwelt on by Keats—"Bards of Passion and of Mirth/Ye have left your souls on earth!" [3]—and the young poet envisions his own verses lending ease to some troubled mind hereafter. The poem is melancholy and sentimental to a degree, "soft" in diction, tone, and attitude. Here is none of the pride and passion with which Shakespeare anticipates the power of his lines over the minds of men unborn, the magnificent arrogance of the poet dreaming of immortality. This youthful poet inhabits a twilight world, a world of nostalgia, heartache, and illness. It is a world of "woe," of "the soul's cry," of "dumb tears," and of "language sweet as sobs." The poem, which goes beyond even the early Keats in its luxuriance of sweet sorrow, reminds us that before Owen's birth the Romantics had become the Decadents and that the world of imagination was peopled by darker spirits than Psyche and the bright Apollo.

Poetry, to this particular young poet, is neither vision nor prophecy in the old grand manner, nor is it

> some more humble lay,
> Familiar matter of today
> Some natural sorrow, loss, or pain
> That has been, and may be again.[4]

He describes his "songs" rather as

> weird reveries:
> Low croonings of a motherless child, in gloom
> Singing his frightened self to sleep, are these.

How has divine poesy fallen from her high estate and all her en-
chantments become merely a nursery spell against neurosis!

II   *Isolation and Loneliness*

This sense of isolation and loneliness, of vague dis-ease and
spiritual anxiety, is met with again and again in Owen's youthful
poems. In part it is an inheritance from the Romantics and perhaps especially from the poets of the 1890's by whom Owen was
also powerfully influenced. But, however traditional the theme and
however conventional and mannered Owen's expression of it,
there is no doubt that it expresses something real and important in
the young poet's nature. It finds its symbol in the ghosts who stalk
through these verses, ghosts who cannot communicate with the
world of the living but are shadowy presences troubling dawn or
twilight. In "The Unreturning," the living man watches in vain for
the return of the "far-gone dead," and sees only

> the indefinite unshapen dawn
> With vacant gloaming, sad as half-lit minds,
> The weak-limned hour when sick men's sighs are drained,

and finds himself dreading "even a heaven with doors so chained."
"The Roads Also" sounds the same note of baffled search for
meaning and communication, of dead with living, of past with
present and future:

> Men remember alien ardours
> As the dusk unearths old mournful odours,
> In the garden unborn child souls wail
> And the dead scribble on walls.

The most successful treatment of the ghost motif is "Shadwell Stair," a haunting little poem which employs the "In Memoriam" stanza but imparts to it a different rhythm altogether—one fluid and rocking with accents less regular and deliberate. In this poem rhythm and diction work together to become true incantation:

> Yet I have flesh both firm and cool,
> And eyes tumultuous as the gems
> Of moons and lamps in the lapping Thames
> When dusk sails wavering down the pool.

Almost as poignant as the ghost's loneliness is that of the frustrated lover seeking his love, seeking Love itself. Like all young men, Owen dreamed of love, of finding "All beauty, once for ever, in one face." [5] But the love he seeks is not one of flesh and blood; for him, Love, like Beauty—which is only another name for Love —is not the satisfaction of the senses, not the enlarging and heightening of experience in the real world. Both Love and Beauty are rather gateways to an ideal world. And this longing for the ideal has its roots in fear, in a shrinking from the exigent conditions of mortal life, in the desire to find a refuge from the inexorable realities of Time and Sorrow. The prominence of this theme links Owen at one end of the century with the early Keats, at the other with the young Yeats of such poems as "The White Birds" and "The Sorrow of Love," and with other poets in between: with William Morris and Algernon Charles Swinburne, with Dante Gabriel Rossetti, with Ernest Dowson and Arthur Symons and Oscar Wilde, with all those poets who had expressed lyrically while they had wrestled unsuccessfully with the nineteenth-century temptations to escapism.

III   Escape from Time and Sorrow

Next to loneliness, escape, in one form or another, is the dominant motif of Owen's early verse. He longs to escape back to early childhood, "the happiness our mother gave us," but knows that "The former happiness is unreturning." [6] Another sonnet, "To a Child," laments, like Wordsworth in his "Intimations of Immortality" ode, that the happy innocence, the "gold" the child brings with him from another sphere, must soon be dulled by the knowledge of this world. The speaker in "My Shy Hand," apparently the goddess Aphrodite, offers to the beloved in place of passion "a hermitage" of timeless peace. She promises not the satisfactions of experience but the consolations of dreams—cushions "for reveries," a pillow "for thy brow's fatigues," and a release from the world of striving and sorrow: "Thither your years may gather in from storm,/And Love, that sleepeth there, will keep thee warm." All lovers have seen love as shield and buckler against the arrows of fortune; but this lover does not contemplate love as the sweetest experience of human life, nor even as solace for life's pains. He longs for a translation from life altogether, a removal from the realm of Becoming to that of Being.

A more successful treatment of the same theme of escape is the sonnet titled "The Fates," in which Beauty rather than Love is the "secret gate" by means of which the poet may foil "those informers to the Fates/Called Fortune, Chance, Necessity, and Death;" and he promises himself that "So I'll evade the vice and rack of age/And miss the march of lifetime, stage by stage." The tone is Shakespeare's, harder and more impersonal than usual in Owen's early poems; and it imparts to the sonnet a sense of decision, a crispness much more tonic than the lush, overripe manner Owen preferred at this time. The theme and attitude, however, are not Shakespearean but belong to that cult of beauty bequeathed by the early to the late nineteenth century and made hypochondriac by the changes of time and fortune. Shakespeare knew, no poet better, the power of Time against which nor brass, nor stone, nor earth, nor boundless sea might contend. Against that devouring rage he set the all-but-divine power of art, of poetry which might make human love immortal; but the Decadents of the late century, and the Georgians who followed, did not do so. They declined the challenge, escaping from the great Shakespearean stage into private closes and gardens. The poet was no longer prophet and bard of a world ranging from Heaven to Hell; he had become, as Morris described himself, "the idle singer of an empty day." It is not strange that Owen, to whose youthful temperament this pretty and melodious escapism appealed so much, should have been their heir. What is strange is that he should so soon have disavowed his inheritance and set out to make his own poetic fortune.

The lover of Owen's youthful imagination does not desire the consummation of an earthly love. He prefers the search for the ideal and the unattainable; and he loves the idea of Love, the abstraction, not a mortal beloved. Keats's Endymion fell in love with Cynthia, the moon-goddess, symbol of ideal Beauty; the young Owen falls in love with Eros, Love himself. "To the Bitter Sweet-heart: a Dream" rejects the mortal lover for whom the poet has searched in favor of the winged god of love who offers himself as a "passion-friend." Summarily, the poet dismisses his former sweetheart:

> So my old quest of you requited is,
> Ampler than e'er I asked of your girl's grace.
> I shall not ask you more, nor see your face.

It is unrealistic as well as unchivalrous to expect any actual girl, whatever her grace, to compete with Cupid for her lover's affections; but realism and chivalry were not at this time Owen's points of strength. We cannot help suspecting that this girl missed very little, however, for even when the poet has found a real live Princess:

> Sojourning through a southern realm in youth,
> I came upon a house by happy chance
> Where bode a marvellous Beauty

he withdraws from her after the first tentative kiss:

> Because it was too soon, and not my part,
> To start voluptuous pulses in her heart,
> And kiss her to the world of Consciousness.[7]

A generation more steeped than Owen's in the lore and language of psychology might be forgiven for murmuring "projection." Whatever voluptuous pulses may have been stirring in his heart, it is clearly the poet himself who has not yet been kissed or cuffed to "the world of consciousness." In fact, the lover he most closely resembles is Bunthorne in W. S. Gilbert's *Patience* who, it will be remembered, describes himself as a "Francesca da Rimini/ Niminy piminy/ Je ne sais quoi young man" and who recommends a prospective lover to attach himself to an object which would certainly not suit most of us:

> Then a sentimental passion of a vegetable fashion
> Must excite your languid spleen,
> An attachment à la Plato to a bashful young potato,
> Or a not-too-French French bean. . . .

If Owen's youthful love poems attest to anything, they do to the accuracy of Gilbert's observations of the literary scene.

The shrinking from the pain of actual experience, from the risks of life and love, implied in such poems as "The Sleeping Beauty" and "To the Bitter Sweet-heart" is more explicit in others. "Sonnet Autumnal" envisages the end of love as bringing "The menace of a drear and mighty storm," the approach of which portends sorrow and suffering; a sonnet all the gloomier in mood for being a deliberate imitation of the grand and gloomy manner of Dante Gabriel Rossetti's "House of Life" sonnet sequence. Rossetti, however, knew the bitter truth of these emotions; he spoke with authority and not as one of the scribes, while the inspiration of Owen's poem is wholly literary. Even more artificial is "To Eros," in which the young man who was too diffident to kiss the Sleeping Beauty to consciousness acknowledges the power and cruelty of the god to whom he has sacrificed all other loves—"Old peaceful lives; frail flowers; firm friends; and Christ"—and who then deserts his worshiper. In another sonnet, "Storm," the poet, in a strange mixture of mythological allusions, imagines himself first as a sort of Ajax drawing down upon himself the lightning of love while the great gods laugh, and then as an Icarus tumbling from heaven, having flown too near the sun.

One untitled sonnet is a refreshing change from this artificial and spurious emotion, these grandiose traditional figures, this self-dramatization. But even in it the air of carefree charm and the apparent lightness of touch are entirely deceptive. Love is imaged as a mischievous child tripping and tumbling two other children at play on a beach:

> We cannot help but fall;
> What matter? Why, it will not hurt at all,
> Our youth is supple, and the world is sand.

But the poet knows better, and cannot wholly deceive even himself. His admonishment to

> mind that we
> Both laugh with love; and having tumbled, try
> To go forever children, hand in hand

is singularly unconvincing—as unconvincing as Peter Pan's similar desire—and the fear that motivates the wish to escape from the real world in which children must grow up peeps out in the final line of the sonnet, sounding a note somber, almost threatening, in its repetition and elision: "The sea is rising . . . and the world is sand." Delightful as he is, Love is a notoriously capricious, unreliable god; and the young poet is uneasily aware that his victims seldom escape so lightly as children frolicking in the sand.

"Song of Songs," first of the four poems to be published in Owen's lifetime, comes comparatively late chronologically, having presumably been composed during the summer of 1917. As his editor, C. Day Lewis, observes, however, it is "interesting as an example of Owen's relapse into the 'poetic' manner of his juvenilia," [8] and chronology aside, it may be treated as one of the early poems. It exhibits, in twelve brief lines, all the most artificial and derivative characteristics of Owen's youthful verse. A whole gallery of nineteenth-century worthies are exhibited in mannerisms of tone and diction, in verbal tricks of vowel and consonant, in a turn of phrase and of thought from Christina Rossetti's "Echo," in an unmistakably Swinburnian cadence, in the "leaflets," and the "viols" of the 1890's of Dowson, Wilde, and Symons. We also find a reminiscence of early Morris and the Pre-Raphaelites; and, echoing from a greater distance, a greater poet, Shelley, who for obvious reasons appealed to Owen almost as much as Keats.

"Song of Songs" is a pastiche, therefore, of all that was most vague and sickly in the nineteenth-century convention of romantic love: sensuousness without passion; emotion for its own sake, lacking a concrete object; the refusal of the real world for a never-never land, half adolescent dream and half Garden of Eden. Technically, the poem is quite accomplished in the rising and falling of its cadences and in the manipulation of long and short, open and close vowel sounds. Otherwise, it stands as an example of all that was lacking in Georgian poetry. "Music," also a relatively late poem, exhibits the same mixture of influences and the same self-conscious and ersatz treatment of the pleasures of both art and love. Did the young man who, not many months later,

wrote proudly to his mother, "I am held peer by the Georgians,"
realize how far his mature poems transcended their limitations?

IV *Early Imagery*

Owen would not have been true to the tradition that so gripped
him had he not now and then played with the possibilities of
sense imagery for its own sake. "Spells and Incantation (a Fragment)" is an exploitation of the sensuous richness of jewel colors,
pearls and diamonds, rubies and amber, each reflecting in turn the
color and atmosphere of the seasons from winter through spring
and summer to autumn. The four stanzas printed in the *Collected
Poems* (others were omitted by the editor as inferior) might have
been written by one of the Imagist poets. "All Sounds have
been as Music" shows him combining reminiscences of Keats's
Sonnet IV with those of Rupert Brooke's "The Great Lover."

The chief interest of "All Sounds . . . ," however, as of "Bugles
Sang," which appears to be another attempt at the same poem, is
the employment of imagery later used with extraordinary effectiveness in Owen's war sonnet "Anthem for Doomed Youth." The
bugles that sadden the air, the appeal of the country bells, the
wailing of shells, and the anger of the guns make a momentary
and uncoordinated appearance but are blended in the later poem
into a triumphant and harmonious whole. The sonnet entitled
"1914" also foreshadows here and there an image to be used in the
later war verse. Juvenile for the most part in phraseology, it exhibits the typical vagueness and abstract quality of Owen's early
work:

> Rent or furled
> Are all Art's ensigns. Verse wails. Now begin
> Famines of thought and feeling. Love's wine's thin

But it employs two figures of speech which later undergo something like an apotheosis; the octave concludes with the line: "The
grain of human Autumn rots, down-hurled." In one of his greatest
poems, "Asleep," Owen remembered this figure. A soldier has
been killed while sleeping, and the poet speculates on "his deeper
sleep" whether it be "High pillowed on calm pillows of God's
making,"

—Or whether yet his thin and sodden head
Confuses more and more with the low mould,
His hair being one with the grey grass
And finished fields of autumns that are old . . .

The direction of Owen's poetic development was from the abstract and the general to the concrete and the particular, the precise and scrupulous choice of the exact word; from the florid and rhetorical flourish of an attitude to the calm perception and acceptance of fact.

The final two lines of the sonnet—"But now for us, wild Winter, and the need/Of sowings for new Spring, and blood for seed"— were obviously suggested by Shelley's "Ode to the West Wind." Later, in "Exposure," Owen returns to this idea to develop it into a suggestion far more complex and subtle. It might be noted in passing that a phrase from "The Fates," already quoted: "And miss the march of lifetime, stage by stage" was used in "Strange Meeting" in a different context and employed for a different purpose. These examples show how effectively Owen could return to and use for his war verse undeveloped images and ideas from earlier and less successful poems.

V *Flowers of Evil*

Now and then the estheticism of Owen's early verses loses its innocence and begins to breathe the perfume of the flowers of evil that Baudelaire and Swinburne cultivated and which grew wild in the gardens of the Decadents. "Long Ages Past" chiefly reveals the influence of the Swinburne of "Faustine," "Dolores," and "Hymn to Proserpine,"—those feverish apostrophes to a love which is associated with cruelty, lust, and sin; where pleasure is three parts pain; and in which the cult of beauty becomes a rejection of conventional morality and religion. The poem celebrates an unspecified deity whose worship is compounded of torture, sexual orgies, and death: a deity "Of wild desire, of pain, of bitter pleasure," the deity of an opium dream in which men find "forgetfulness of God." All the stock properties of self-conscious pagan estheticism are here: the jewels, the harps and timbrels, the rich color words, the sado-masochism (though Owen's "on thy lips the stain of crimson blood" is a feeble and mundane rendering of

Swinburne's voluptuous "On thy mouth, though the kisses be bloody");[9] and the arbitrary divorce between God—the Christian God—and the world of the senses and the flesh.

Owen is hardly the first to have found this mixture a heady one; indeed, of the poets of this period, only Hardy seems to have been totally immune to it. Our Lady of Pain has seduced many young men, not all of them poets; and, though the Christ of the Gospels would appear to have had little in common with Swinburne's pale Galilean, there are moods in which it is satisfactory to picture Him thus. Given the apparent choice, what young man would not declare himself in favor of "the breasts of the nymph in the brake"?[10] We are glad, in fact, to know that the timorous lover of "The Sleeping Beauty" sometimes had naughtier impulses. Swinburne is, after all, an intoxicating poet: no one has ever mixed these ingredients with a surer hand, though such later triumphs of the kind as Wilde's "Salome" and "The Sphinx" and James Elroy Flecker's "Hassan" are almost as authoritative.

"The Kind Ghosts" is, at first glance, inspired by the same models and appears to exhibit the same motifs. The poem is late—it is dated July 30, 1918—and presents a curious mixture of Owen's youthful and mature styles. We are back with the ghosts of earlier poems, those presences which can be sensed but who do not communicate with the world of the living: the phantoms of boys slain refrain from haunting the palace of the pagan goddess who has sacrificed them, not wishing to disturb or grieve her. The diction in part recalls Owen's juvenile lushness: "golden gardens and sweet glooms," as does in part the imagery, again reminiscent of Swinburne: "Not marvelling why her roses never fall/Nor what red mouths were torn to make their blooms."

But 1918 was the last year of Owen's life; and there is more than a suggestion that the motive of this poem comes from the real world, not from imagination or from poetry itself; that the pagan goddess here is Bellona, not Proserpine or Dolores; and that the "wall of boys on boys and dooms on dooms," the "hecatombs" of these victims, had been seen by the poet on the Western Front. There is a quietness and control, a restraint, which contrasts vividly with the hectic, almost hysterical tone of "Long Ages Past"; a restraint lent partly by the rhyme scheme and stanza form and partly by the choice, for the most part, of matter-of-fact, everyday words rather than the exotic vocabulary, the straining after effect which characterizes the earlier poem.

These "kind" ghosts who will not trouble the sleep of their slayer have something in common with those in the war poem "Exposure" who, having sought their homes and those for whom they must die, "turn back to our dying." The neurotic loneliness and isolation in the early poems, the loneliness of an ego absorbed in itself and unable to communicate with others, has become the more real but more meaningful isolation of those who must lay down their lives for the sake of others, and who love with a "greater love" that precludes hate. Pagan estheticism which, with Owen, had never amounted to more than a youthful trying on of a particular role, as in boyhood he had tried on the role of priest, has yielded to an image of real, not imagined, cruelty and sin and a love that has nothing in common with lust. Particularly impressive is the awareness of the victims and their acceptance of their fate, by contrast with the serenely unaware cruelty of the deity to whom they have been sacrificed. The poem is a curious marriage of later insights with earlier fantasies. In its technical skill it reveals the mature poet: the interplay of vowels and the deft repetition of rhymes show an easy mastery free from strain; and the manuscript is marked to indicate alliteration and internal rhyme, evidence of the poet's attention to these details.

VI *Dreams of Fame*

Young poets are apt to dream of fame, as well as of love and beauty. Several of Owen's early verses express not only the traditional hope for immortality through poetry but the young man's as yet unconfirmed conviction that he is one of a glorious fellowship of choice spirits set apart from ordinary mortals. "Poets," Shelley had said, "are the unacknowledged legislators of mankind," and the "Ode to the West Wind" concludes with a prayer that, by the incantation of verse, the poet's dead thoughts may be driven over the universe to be the trumpet of a prophecy and to quicken a new birth. "O World of Many Worlds" owes much to Shelley's inspiration, but in diction and phrasing it recalls less the magnificent ode than the feebler and more extravagant effusions of a somewhat uneven poet.

Picturing himself at first as lost amid the "loud machinery" of the universe, "Fainting by violence of the Dance"—much as Shelley was fond of picturing himself as falling on the thorns of life, or as a "herd-abandoned deer struck by the hunter's dart"—the poet recovers his equilibrium on a vantage point from which he can contemplate, godlike, the swarming masses of humanity. Each is isolated from his fellows; each follows "destinies foreplanned" and is bound by laws which he must blindly obey. "I would not step with such a band," says the young poet:

> To be a meteor, fast, eccentric, lone,
> Lawless; in passage through all spheres,
> Warning the earth of wider ways unknown
> And rousing men with heavenly fears—
>
> This is the track reserved for my endeavour;

Momentarily he trembles at this prospect, but he allays his fears and concludes the poem by recalling "other wandering souls" who "are lights unto themselves," and who are "greater than this system's sun" when in after times they return with their "self-radiated aureoles" to earth.

This jejune example of Romantic self-dramatization and egotism would not be worth noticing but for the striking contrast it makes with Owen's later views of poetry and of his own function as poet. "All a poet can do today is warn," he said in the Preface to the volume of war poems he planned during the last months of his life. The later warning was not to be "of wider ways unknown" but of the terrible realities of known ways of modern war, and the poet saw himself no longer as a lawless meteor following his own paths and scorning the foreplanned destinies of common men; he was now a participant in and spokesman for the suffering, the sacrifice, and the guilt of humanity.

The next time the poet imagines himself high above the world, surveying the masses below, his soul is looking down "from a vague height, with Death," at the horror of the Western Front. Across that awful landscape swarms of caterpillars are eating and being eaten, and Death shows the poet "a manner of worm" which has "the feet of many men," but whose fresh-severed head is his own. No longer was he isolated or set apart, but identified as closely as possible with suffering and sinful men.

"Training," like "The Kind Ghosts" a late poem, is a treatment of the poet's vision of fame altogether more successful than "O World of Many Worlds." More terse and compact than most of the early verses, it is controlled by its rhyme scheme, a variation of terza rima in which the third and last stanza repeats the *aba* pattern of the first, and by its single image of the athlete striving for the traditional laurel crown. All other goals, and the pleasures of love in particular, must yield to the one aim of glory:

> Cold winds encountered on the racing Down
> Shall thrill my heated bareness; but awhile
> None else may meet me till I wear my crown.

Harold Owen, in his autobiography, recalls a conversation with Wilfred during one of their rare meetings on leave in wartime. The elder brother confessed to the younger that he "liked all young women very much," but that he had neither time nor energy to spare for them. They would, he said, distract him from the pursuit of writing his poetry; and his time was all too short. "What else matters?" he concluded.[11] "Training" carries a note of conviction and sincerity that the more florid and self-conscious "O World of Many Worlds" lacks.

VII   *From Dreams to Reality*

Some of the best criticism of Owen's poetry has come from France, and we may therefore be well advised to listen to Frenchmen when they speak of it.

He [Owen] was compelled, because of his noble aim, to sacrifice all the traditions and ideals he cherished. . . . He should have been a poet of peace and beauty, of exquisite raptures and subtle questionings, a delicate painter of miniatures. He had already achieved distinction here, and gained recognition as one of the sweetest voices of his generation. . . . To the end, the direct unconventional violence—what we may call the modern element—in his war-verse remained alien to him, outraged his deepest instincts and beliefs. He was naturally a lover of tradition, a belated Victorian. Through the emotional reaction the war aroused in him, he was exalted above himself, above his normal poetic stature. Fate used him with bitter irony indeed, since he is bound to live in the memories of men mainly as a war-poet. His fame rests on poems torn from him. . . . To him, indeed, his war-poems did not count, they were emphatically not poetry.[12]

A careful reading of the early poems makes it difficult to agree with M. Loiseau that the war poems represent a loss of Owen's true poetic world. "He had preserved inviolate his poetic ideal, and set it quite apart from the ruggedness and vehemence of his war-poems. Poetry must be 'poetical' in the traditional sense, a delicate feast for the intellect, the senses, the ear. . . ." [13] Certainly, as we have seen, this was the younger Owen's conception of poetry. His early poetry reveals him as a natural Romantic; but it reveals also how anemic the Romantic tradition had become, and how adolescent was Owen's expression of it. He would have remained a painter of miniatures indeed had he lingered in that enclosed garden.

The key to Owen's achievement of poetic maturity is his discovery of the inadequacy of his former poetic creed to express the realities of contemporary experience, and his decision to grapple with those realities rather than escape through the traditional gates of Love and Beauty to a world of fantasy. Because he found "poetry," like "religion," inadequate for a man who wished to see and to speak the truth, he was compelled to adopt a deliberately "anti-poetic" attitude. "The poet," observed Wordsworth, "is a man speaking to men." Owen had come to agree with that view. The voice which at first had been that of a motherless child "Singing his frightened self to sleep" had become a man's voice speaking to men with calm assurance. In his great poems, it became more: a voice that spoke with the ancient authority of priest and prophet.

At least two of the juvenilia, neither of great merit, point the way to what was happening to this heretofore rather Ninetyish young man. "Bold Horatius" presents a teacher who "bleats" Macaulay's "Lays of Ancient Rome," a Victorian paean to the martial valor of the past, but who will not speak to actual real-life soldiers: "One was called 'Orace whom she would not greet." The poet himself makes no comment on this confrontation of "poetry" with reality; and no comment is necessary. The other poem, "Maundy Thursday," is one of Owen's many sonnets. It has, C. Day Lewis tells us, "an edge of truthfulness, an unconventionality, and a self-revelation which make it the most impressive of Owen's juvenilia." [14] At worship in church, the poet kisses not the figure of Christ on the proffered crucifix but instead "the warm live hand that held the thing."

Neither of these poems can be dated with any certainty, but it is not important that they should be. What they tell us clearly is that Owen had found the poetry and the religion of his boyhood and youth inadequate to the experiences, the emotions, and the demands of maturity. It is not true that his war verse "outraged his deepest instincts and beliefs." It was "poetry" and "religion" that outraged them. He did not "sacrifice all the traditions and ideals he cherished." He disavowed them when he found that they did not square with the truth of his experiences, nor allow him to speak it. Owen's real voice is not the one that sounds in the feverish fantasies of his juvenilia. It is time to listen to the voice of the true poet he became, in so short a time and at such a cost.

CHAPTER 3

The Pity of War

WITH Owen's war poems we enter a world so different from the poetic world of his juvenilia that it is often difficult to believe these verses were produced by the same young man who wrote "On My Songs." The difference is not simply that of subject; it is fundamentally one of perspective and of purpose. These poems reflect the changes that had taken place within the poet as well as in the outer world, changes of attitude toward himself and others, and most particularly a change in his poetic goals. The attainment of verbal beauty, though he often attained it, was no longer Owen's aspiration. Nor did he write, as he had earlier, to console himself, to express and discharge his own emotions: "easing the flow/Of my dumb tears with language sweet as sobs." His hope of fame, though it persisted, had become secondary to a motive more pressing.

The war poems were written to tell the truth about modern war, as it had not been told before: to warn England and the world of what men were doing to one another. They were designed with all deliberation to be propaganda. The role of the poet, as Owen now saw it, was to warn; to see and, speaking, to make others see. Not personal satisfaction, nor beauty, but truth was now to be his master, and all his poetic powers were directed to expressing the meaning of the new truth with which he must come to terms: his experience of war. Vision and craftsmanship alike were at the service of a purpose neither personal nor artistic but moral. Having seen the trenches, he could no longer linger in the Palace of Art.

To call Owen's war poetry propaganda does not mean that it preaches either creed or dogma nor that it concentrates exclusively upon the immediate facts of his situation. Except when carried away by anger and contempt, as he was now and then, he does not preach at all. His is poetry not of exhortation or of mes-

sage but of vision. And the range of his vision extends far beyond
the bloodshed and the agonies he re-creates so vividly. Owen's
desire to expose the traditional "noble" and "poetic" view of war
naturally involved the depiction of horrors; and the realities of
death, mutilation, and madness are concretely present in his war
poems. Although he does not let us forget them for an instant,
these horrors are not dwelt upon for their own sake: they are
there to serve a vision. And the vision itself encompasses both the
particular facts of war and universal and fundamental ones of human experience.

Not the present only but also the past and the future are implicit in Owen's best poems. Their background is historical time,
evolutionary time, and eternity. He speaks of what it meant to be
a soldier on the Western Front during World War I, and also of
what it means to be a man. At his best, he is not a realistic but an
imaginative poet, a prophet and a myth-maker. And even his
more realistic poems seldom remain merely descriptive; they
move always from the facts of outer experience to interpretation.
Not the event itself but its implication, its inner meaning, is what
matters—and not only to victim or observer but to all men: "His
images burst into symbols before our eyes, and we feel, not the
harshness of individual suffering, so much as the tragedy of universal pain." [1]

I *The Meaning of Pity*

The key to an appreciation of Owen's war poetry is an understanding of the term "pity," a term he used in his Preface without
definition or discussion, but which has been variously discussed
and defined by others: "My subject is War and the pity of War.
The Poetry is in the pity." The truth of the poem, that is, lies in
the truth and power of the emotion it expresses and evokes, in the
response appropriate to and arising from the treatment of incident
or situation. The poet must see clearly, feel vividly and honestly,
and re-create his experience for the reader with poetic power; or
there can be no true response and therefore no true poetry.
"Above all I am not concerned with Poetry," wrote Owen. "Poetry" he rejected because he felt it falsified both fact and emotion.
But he would write of war and the pity of war, and in the pity of
war was the poetry.

Most of the negative criticism of Owen's poems has stemmed

from too narrow an interpretation of his term "pity," or from what sometimes seems like wilful failure to understand what he meant. The best known instance is the exclusion of Owen from the *Oxford Book of Modern Verse* which W. B. Yeats edited in 1936. "Passive suffering," said Yeats, "is not a theme for poetry." [2] In a private letter written in 1924, but not published until 1942, Sir Henry Newbolt, himself a war poet of a more traditional type, spoke for those who interpret pity in a narrow and partial sense:

> Sassoon has sent me Wilfred Owen's Poems, with an introduction by himself. The best of them I knew already—they are terribly good, but of course limited, almost all on one note. I like better Sassoon's two-sided collection—there are more than two sides to this business of war, and a man is hardly normal any longer if he comes down to one. S. S. says that Owen pitied others but never himself: I'm afraid that isn't quite true—or at any rate not quite fair. To be a man one must be willing that others as well as yourself should bear the burden that must be borne.[3]

Other critics have followed Yeats's lead. Nearly thirty years after the *Oxford Book of Modern Verse*, a study of modern poetry quotes his judgment with approval: "to make as much of this anemic emotion as Owen did is to run the danger of producing poems which are 'all blood, dirt, and sucked sugar stick' [Yeats's description of Owen's war poems] . . . pity is without meaning unless the poet controls his material." [4] Even a friendlier critic echoes the same condemnation: "Except in circumstances of catastrophic accident, or of resignation to a predestined fate, pity is not an adequate emotion in poetry. It tends to become negative, exhausting, sentimental, masochistic. . . ." [5]

There are grounds for criticism, or at least for question, of some of the attitudes and sentiments Owen expresses; but of this objection to pity as a proper theme for poetry it must be said that these critics have failed to read the poems Owen wrote. Even if the dictum itself should be accepted without argument, passive suffering is not the theme of Owen's war poetry; and his pity, though it includes anguish and anger at suffering, means something far more profound.

In Owen's greatest poems it becomes clear that he sees war as the

microcosm and symbol of the universal tragedy of human life—
a tragedy enacted in the trenches of his particular present situation, in the remote past, and to be enacted in the future too.
Suffering and waste, violence and evil are the necessary conditions of human life. These are elegies for his own generation and
for men in all times and places. They are elegies for the earth
herself, subject to the same cosmic necessities, to suffering and
grief, to the changes of time and decay.

In one of his finest sonnets, "The End," Owen summons a vision
of the Judgment Day, announced significantly in military terms:
"After the drums of time have rolled and ceased,/And by the
bronze west long retreat is blown," and asks the great question
posed by the Lord to the prophet Ezekiel, "Can these bones
live?" [6]: "Shall Life renew these bodies? Of a truth/All death will
he annul, all tears assuage?"—But the poet does not return the
prophet's answer, "O Lord God, thou knowest." Nor does he, like
John of Revelation, see "a new heaven and a new earth: for the
first heaven and the first earth were passed away; and there was
no more sea." [7] Instead, Earth replies: "Mine ancient scars shall
not be glorified,/Nor my titanic tears, the seas, be dried."

"Miners," one of Owen's few fine poems not specifically on the
topic of war, conjures up in fantasy the age-old process by which
coal is produced deep in the earth, at a great cost, to warm future
generations, analogizing the miner's fate to that of the soldier:

> The centuries will burn rich loads
> With which we groaned,
> Whose warmth shall lull their dreaming lids
> While songs are crooned.
> But they will not dream of us poor lads
> Lost in the ground.

In these and in other poems Owen transcends the limitations of
time and place, by depth of emotion and verbal mastery and even
more by virtue of his perspective. He writes of war; and some of
his poems, chiefly the less successful ones, treat particular aspects
of his particular conflict. But his best verses are not captive in and
limited by a special, and especially abnormal, situation. He sees
the tragedy of war in the long context of human history or against

the backdrop of eternity. Owen's is neither a limited nor a sentimental vision. Like the great tragic poets, he sees the splendor
and beauty of life, the potentialities for grandeur of the human
spirit, and the inevitability of suffering and death. And the great
and constant theme of his poems is neither passive suffering nor
death itself. It is the tragic contrast between potentiality and ac-
tuality, what might be and what is.

War to Owen is the immediate and vivid instance of a more
fundamental tragedy: the inhumanity of man, his brutal denial of
human values, his annihilation of human potentialities. The suffering of which he writes is as much the suffering of guilt, the searing
of the souls of men by the violence they do others, as it is the
passive suffering of the victims of violence. He pities the dead
because they are dead, and the living because they must live with
the knowledge of guilt and evil. Even worse, perhaps, is the plight
of those who have become dehumanized, who are too selfish and
callous to understand tragedy, too insensible to identify with
suffering. Life and love, physical beauty and spiritual innocence,
the universal bond of sympathy and brotherhood, all that it means
to be truly human: these are assaulted, degraded, denied, destroyed by war. It is the very sign and seal of an evil which in-
volves all men, willy-nilly, which blasts all good with wanton ma-
lignance; and, after it, the survivors face the future with souls
besmirched with blood, or deprived of their own humanity as well
as of the salvation that might have been offered them by those
who died.

The meaning of "pity" to Owen, then, must be understood in
this more universal sense. Profoundly aware of the inevitable
tragedy of man's fate in the universe, seeing all men bound by
common bonds of sympathy and love, and facing a common end,
he was as profoundly convinced that man's nature is creation, not
destruction. His protest against war was thus a protest against
war's deliberate reversal of all the values that men should uphold.
It is an evil committed always and everywhere against humanity
itself. This theme, this viewpoint, underlies and conditions all of
Owen's mature poetry, whatever the particular subject of individual poems. The only just and worthwhile war, he feels, would be
one in the service of humanity; and in "The Next War" he visual-
izes a time when men may war together on Death, rather than
each other:

We laughed, knowing that better men would come,
And greater wars; when each proud fighter brags
He wars on Death—for lives; not men—for flags.

Meanwhile, however, war is a crime against man's very nature
and being, a reversal of the order of creation itself.

II *The Violation of Nature*

The theme of war as a violation of nature and of natural processes is treated in several of Owen's finest poems. These tend to be
less factual than imaginative or visionary interpretations of fact,
and are usually built up of contrasts and comparisons which make
this reversal of values vivid and explicit. "Asleep" makes its central point in one swift and striking image: the death of a soldier
while asleep is described; the actual act of his dying, as well as the
fact of his death. This act is presented in terms of unnatural child-
birth: the soldier's body, which has been possessed of life as a
woman's body is possessed of her unborn child, is delivered, as it
were, of life by the bullet that kills him, as the woman might be
delivered of her child by abortion. The result in both cases is unnatural death by violent interference with creative processes. War
is an offense against the natural order; and in the final image of
the stanza the soldier's blood, like a live creature, creeps out to
investigate the intrusion of this alien violence.

"Futility," as perfect a poem as Owen ever wrote, makes the
same point but in a much larger perspective. It is woven of a
whole series of correspondences and antitheses: present and past,
man and Nature, purposeful endeavor and futility, creation and
destruction. The focus of the poem is less on the particular fact of
the soldier's death than on the implication of that fact for all the
cosmos. In this, too, it is akin to "Asleep," the final thrust of which
is that the living who must continue to take part in such senseless
violence are more to be pitied than the dead.

"Futility" opens with the present reality—the dead soldier in
the snow of France—and in a mood of what sounds like controlled hope, with the speaker's command, "Move him into the
sun." The sun, symbol of life and light, of the creative powers of
the universe, has always awakened the youth to his task of sowing
the seeds of new life. Long before his birth, the sun summoned
the cold earth to life, mothering all things born. Only yesterday

the youth himself was "dear-achieved," wakened to life by the
creative love of man and woman, the crown and justification of
the whole long process of evolution. Now that which life had
toiled to bring to birth lies dead in battle, creator turned destroyer
and himself destroyed; and his death makes hideous mockery of
all creation: "dear-achieved" is contrasted in the penultimate line
with the master stroke, "fatuous": "—O what made fatuous sunbeams toil/To break earth's sleep at all?" But it is man's fatuity
that has reversed the order of nature and blasphemed against the
lord of life, and the lamentation of the living is less for the dead
man, or for themselves personally, than for the futility of all creation in the face of war.

Implicit in many of Owen's poems is the sense of a mysterious
bond between men and Nature. In violating their own human
nature, in reversing by violence the natural order, men alienate
themselves from Nature herself. Their dehumanization is shown
often in terms of this alienation. The unnaturalness of war is reflected in their view of natural phenomena; Nature herself is
affected by and echoes their violence; and men in battle or dying
of wounds console themselves with dreams of another, kinder Nature with which once they were in tune and which they may again
rejoin in death.

"Insensibility" shows soldiers whose senses as well as their souls
have been damaged until they can no longer perceive or respond
normally to the world about them:

> Having seen all things red,
> Their eyes are rid
> Of the hurt of the colour of blood for ever.

A step beyond this are the disordered minds of the mad soldiers in
"Mental Cases," who see all natural phenomena in terms of blood:
"Sunlight seems a blood-smear; night comes blood-black;/Dawn
breaks open like a wound that bleeds afresh." In "Conscious," a
young soldier dying in hospital is helped back to consciousness by
the yellow mayflowers at his head; but he lapses into a delirium
shot with images of battle confused with earlier experiences of
beauty and peace: "Music and roses burst through crimson
slaughter./He can't remember where he saw blue sky." Departing
troops in "The Send-Off" mock the meaning of the flowers given

them by women, thus converting a tribute of love to the living into a gesture of grief and farewell to the dead; and this parody is a symbol of the unnaturalness of the whole war situation: "Their breasts were stuck all white with wreath and spray/As men's are, dead."

The cold, dazed, and weary men of "Exposure" see dawn in terms of a German attack: "Dawn massing in the east her melancholy army/Attacks once more in ranks on shivering ranks of gray . . ." Cowering in their snow-filled trenches, they dream of a kinder past they once knew when Nature was not hostile but a friend:

> We cringe in holes, back on forgotten dreams, and stare
>   snow-dazed
> Deep into grassier ditches. So we drowse, sun-dozed,
> Littered with blossoms trickling where the blackbird fusses.

In "A Terre" and "Spring Offensive" the relationship and bond of sympathy between man and Nature, breached by war, is the theme of the poem. The mutilated and dying officer of "A Terre" pleads:

>   God! For one year—
> To help myself to nothing more than air!
> One Spring! Is one too good to spare, too long?
> Spring wind would work its own way to my lung,
> And grow me legs as quick as lilac-shoots.

He consoles himself with the reflection:

> I shall be better off with plants that share
> More peaceably the meadow and the shower.
> Soft rains will touch me,—as they could touch once,
> And nothing but the sun shall make me ware.
> Your guns may crash around me. I'll not hear;
> . . . .
> Soldiers may grow a soul when turned to fronds,
> But here the thing's best left at home with friends.

"Spring Offensive," one of Owen's subtlest and most suggestive poems, is poignant with the sense of two worlds, the natural

world friendly to man in which men are at home, and the mysterious menace and hostility of that world in war. The poem opens
with a peaceful and meditative interlude, full of the sense of the
healing power of nature. The summer "oozed into their veins/
Like an injected drug for their bodies' pains"; the buttercup has
blessed their boots with gold; the little brambles cling to them
"like sorrowing hands"; and they themselves, a part of this benefi-
cence, "breathe like trees unstirred." But even in this interlude the
sky is stark and blank, indefinably threatening: "Sharp on their
souls hung the imminent line of grass,/Fearfully flashed the sky's
mysterious glass . . ." When the alarm is given and they turn
from the bounty of the sun, rejecting the life-giving power of nature to enter battle, sky and earth return violence for violence:

> And instantly the whole sky burned
> With fury against them; earth set sudden cups
> In thousands for their blood; and the green slope
> Chasmed and steepened sheer to infinite space.

At the end of the poem we are left not so much with the dead as
with the effect of battle on the survivors. Those who have

> . . . rushed in the body to enter hell,
> And there out-fiending all its fiends and flames
> With superhuman inhumanities,
> Long-famous glories, immemorial shames—
> And crawling slowly back, have by degrees
> Regained cool peaceful air in wonder—

find themselves unable even to lament: "Why speak not they of
comrades that went under?" Having rejected the beauty and healing of nature and their own humanity by entering battle, they
return unfitted for any affirmation, for any reaction except simple
wonder at their own survival.

The unnaturalness of man's use of weapons is the theme of
"Arms and the Boy," one of Owen's finest poems. The innocence,
the helplessness, and the beauty of youth are contrasted with the
destructive power and malignity of the arms of war. In this poem,
as in "Futility" and in "Asleep," the poet implies that man is intended by nature for love and creation, not destruction. Nature
does not equip him for combat; for, unlike the tiger, the hawk, or

the stag, he possesses no weapons of his own with which to make war on his fellows; and only by denying and distorting his humanity can he fit himself for battle. So pathetically helpless is he in mechanized warfare, so great is the contrast between his human nature and the inhuman machines of war, that this essential incongruity becomes a gigantic and devilish joke, a joke played on flesh and blood by arms and relished by them. In "Arms and the Boy," the bayonet blade is "thinly drawn with famishing for flesh," and bullets "long to nuzzle in the hearts of lads": they have a kind of human inhumanity, like villains of melodrama. But in "The Last Laugh" weapons mock human love, human fear, and the grisly joke of this helpless creature waging war:

> The Bullets chirped—In vain! vain! vain!
> Machine-guns chuckled,—Tut-tut! Tut-tut!
> And the Big Gun guffawed.
>
> .   .   .   .
> And the lofty Shrapnel-cloud
> Leisurely gestured,—Fool!
> And the falling splinters tittered.

"Disabled" is the ghastly picture of the final end of this unequal collision: the multiple amputee forever cut off from life and love, condemned to an existence not human any longer but—except for his anguish—merely vegetable.

III   *Brotherhood, Sacrifice, and Guilt*

If war does violence to the creative order of nature and alienates man from her, it isolates him still more from his own nature, his humanity. Despite Owen's view of man as part of physical nature, bound by natural laws, he also sees him as a spiritual being; and he is subject, therefore, to laws other than those of physical life and growth. One of these laws is the fundamental bond of sympathy and brotherhood between men; and war's effect on the souls of men, separated from identification with their fellows, is as great a blasphemy as its effect on their bodies. Like Donne before him and Hemingway after, Owen insists that "no man is an island, entire of itself," but that all men are involved with each other and that every man's death diminishes his fellows.

This concept is part of what "pity" means: to empathize with the pain of others is to acknowledge that all men are members one of another. To refuse to identify with suffering is to lose an essential part of one's humanity. "Insensibility" is a profound poetic statement of Owen's view that the worst thing that can happen to a man is to be dead to this sense of his oneness with all men, with all suffering, and with all grief. The soldier must lose imagination, retreat into dull insensibility; for soldiers "have enough to carry with ammunition." In so doing, he loses the best part of himself, "Alive, he is not vital overmuch;/Dying, not mortal overmuch;"— but he has no option. He does not choose this spiritual death; he is a victim of the circumstances of war. But of those who, without the soldier's reason and excuse, consciously and deliberately choose not to identify with all suffering, past, present, and future, the poet says:

> But cursed are dullards whom no cannon stuns,
> That they should be as stones;
> Wretched are they, and mean
> With paucity that never was simplicity.
> By choice they made themselves immune
> To pity and whatever mourns in man
> Before the last sea and the hapless stars;
> Whatever mourns when many leave these shores;
> Whatever shares
> The eternal reciprocity of tears.

"The eternal reciprocity of tears": this is Owen's most memorable and moving expression of his theme of pity, the knowledge and the confession of a universal bond.

Closely related to this theme of brotherhood are two other subjects basic to the war poems: the twin themes of sacrifice and of guilt. From the chaos and madness, the desolation and death of war, a great spiritual value may be wrung—the "greater love" of those who sacrifice themselves for others. Again and again Owen treats the suffering of soldiers as sacrifice, an oblation for the sins of others, for the sins of the world. And in his great visionary poems he makes it clear that, whatever particular scapegoats he may seek at times, all men are involved, in the final analysis, in guilt; all are responsible for sin and pain; all are in some way blind, insensible, or helpless to do good and avoid evil. Far from excepting himself from the general indictment, he specifically acknowledges his own share in guilt, identifying with the victims and with the oppressors too, with the slain and with the slayers.

Owen's treatment of these two themes reflects his religious up-bringing and his deeply religious temperament. Despite his rejec-tion of dogma, his was a profoundly religious mind, and all his most characteristic poems are marked by an essentially spiritual element. Not his general outlook alone but the very terms and images he habitually employs are part of the Christian tradition, drawn from Bible and prayer book; and the extent to which the figure of Christ had laid hold of his imagination is reflected in His appearance as person and symbol in poem after poem. This spirit-uality and this specifically Christian orientation, perhaps more than any other one difference, set his poetry apart from that of his fellow war poets. But these poems also reflect even more vividly his rejection of orthodox dogma and of conventional attitudes to-ward the Church and Christianity.

The sacrificial role of the soldier is again and again analogized to that of Christ. In wartime, when Church and State alike deny Christ, He is still present in the love and suffering of soldiers who, like Him, lay down their lives without hate for the sake of others. Sometimes the analogy is only suggested in the terms in which the misery of soldiers is presented; occasionally, it is made wholly ex-plicit.

"Exposure" is at once a vivid and realistic description of the physical and mental suffering of men in the winter trenches and a powerful symbolic statement of the soldier's "imitation of Christ." Visiting in spirit their homes and those for whom they are offering their lives, they find the doors closed on them and turn back to their dying:

> Since we believe not otherwise can kind fires burn;
> Nor ever suns smile true on child, or field, or fruit.
> For God's invincible spring our love is made afraid;
> Therefore, not loath, we lie out here; therefore were born,
> For love of God seems dying.

The fires of war are those that consumed Sodom and Gomorrah, a divine judgment for sin. Like Christ, the soldiers must die for others in order to insure "kind fires," those of household and fam-ily love. Their sacrifice will restore love among all men and the renewed love of God for the world—the fires of redemption, not

the flames of war and hell. But spring will bring Easter and the
Resurrection only after the Crucifixion. God so loved the world
that he gave Christ to redeem it; now, in the new winter of the
world and the soul, mortal men must offer themselves as a sacrifice so that God's love may again live in the world.

Another powerful treatment of this theme is "Greater Love";
like "Futility," this poem is a successful embodiment of a great
subject in brief poetic compass. Again like "Futility," it turns on a
basic contrast, one between sexual love and sacrificial death in
battle. In a series of images, ironic and terrible comparisons are
offered:

> Red lips are not so red
>   As the stained stones kissed by the English dead.
> . . . .
> Your slender attitude
>   Trembles not exquisite like limbs knife-skewed,
>   . . . . . .
> Heart, you were never hot
>   Nor large, nor full like hearts made great with shot.

The poem's great impact is achieved by its repeated juxtapositions
of the physical beauty and desirability of a girl's body with its
promise of sensual love and the ugliness and agony of a soldier's
death. The implication is that the "greater love" his death symbol-
izes and affirms not only far outweighs but renders cheap and
tawdry the values of physical love and all the normal goods and
goals of the flesh. The last stanza specifically identifies the soldier
with Christ, through imagery and allusion to a verse from Luke's
account of the Crucifixion:

> And though your hand be pale,
> Paler are all which trail
> Your cross through flame and hail:
>   Weep, you may weep, for you may touch them not.

The Biblical verse recollected in the last line runs thus:

> And there followed him a great company of people, and of
> women, which also bewailed and lamented him.
> But Jesus turning unto them said, Daughters of Jerusalem,
> weep not for me, but weep for yourselves, and for your children.

> For behold, the days are coming, in the which they shall say,
> Blessed are the barren, and the wombs that never bare, and the
> paps which never gave suck.[8]

The poem suggests an austere rejection of self-fulfillment and of all the material values that life offers and an affirmation that the highest values are those of the spirit gained through sacrifice for others. The issue of the love of man and woman is new life; the result of the soldier's "greater love" is physical death; but out of the hate and violence of war may emerge an enlargement of the spirit more precious than ordinary human life and love. So "Apologia Pro Poemate Meo" in specifically religious terms describes the foul-mouthed Tommies as purified through the offering of themselves as sacrifices:

> Faces that used to curse me, scowl for scowl,
> Shine and lift up with passion of oblation,
> Seraphic for an hour; though they were foul;

and it declares that in the hell of war may be found a love and laughter, a beauty and peace, a glimpse of God, unknown to peacetime and only to be experienced by those who share "With them in hell the sorrowful dark of hell."

Pure Christianity, to Owen, was precisely this spirit of love and sacrifice; and he felt strongly that it was to be found in wartime only among soldiers, having been betrayed and abandoned by the Church. Because those who called themselves Christ's servants had forgotten his commandment of love, he indicts in many of his poems official Christianity for treason to its Founder and for allegiance instead to the bloodthirsty powers of the State; and he contrasts the cruelty, hypocrisy, and indifference of the Church's representatives with the greater love of soldiers. "At a Calvary Near the Ancre" makes this point explicit in its identification of the mutilated figure of the church Christ with the soldiers who "bear with Him," and accuses His disciples of cowardice, His priests and scribes of pride, cruelty, and loyalty to "the Beast/By whom the gentle Christ's denied." "Le Christianisme" strikes a drier, more acrid note:

> So the church Christ was hit and buried
> Under its rubbish and its rubble.

> In cellars, packed-up saints lie serried,
> Well out of hearing of our trouble.

War has literally "buried" Christ; and the Church has wrapped itself, like its well-protected plaster saints, in hypocrisy and indifference to the men for whom He died.

The suggestion that the Christian religion has proven inadequate to the realities of war, that its doctrine and ritual are empty of meaning and consolation for human suffering, is the theme of a far greater poem, "Anthem for Doomed Youth." Like "Futility" and "Greater Love," this sonnet works through a series of contrasts to suggest the negation of all the values of ordinary peaceful life by the facts of war, and especially war's negation of Christianity. The basic opposition is between conventional religious rites of death at home in peacetime and the mockery of these rites by the weapons of war. The bells, the prayers, the songs of Christian death are parodied by the guns and shells; the candles, funeral palls, and flowers of dead soldiers are to be found only in the grief of those bereaved by their deaths.

The power of the poem lies both in the justness and aptness of its images, and in its strong suggestion that customary religious rituals and symbols would now be mockery for the deaths of these "who die as cattle." It is not, in fact, the death of helpless youth that is being mocked by the weapons of war so much as the religion of peacetime which is now seen to be impotent and meaningless. The suggestive power of imagery and symbol in this poem is far more effective in its implicit criticism of the inadequacy of the Church and Christianity than the explicit statement of "At a Calvary" or "Le Christianisme." And the gravity and lofty elegiac tone have much more weight and impact than the irony and anger of the lesser poems. The suggestion of the sestet that human love and human grief are still valid frees the sonnet from any tinge of bitterness such as faintly flavors the conclusion of "Greater Love." A wholly successful poem, "Anthem for Doomed Youth," is perhaps the best that Owen wrote.

IV   *Soldier and Civilian*

Owen's indictment of the Church is given a hard edge by his conviction that the fighting man alone, in wartime, exemplifies

Christianity's true spirit of love and sacrifice. But it is not solely the Church and its representatives who feel the sharp sting of his satire. Like all men on active service, Owen was oppressed by a sense of the great gulf between soldier and noncombatant. Fighting men felt that those who were safe at home could neither understand nor care about their agony. Other poets, like Sassoon, expressed this bitter sense of alienation in their poetry, for example in Sassoon's "Base Details" and "Blighters"; ordinary men gave vent to it in their letters and talk among themselves. It was an essential part of the literature and atmosphere of the war. The bitterness included the official representatives of Church and State, authority figures in the older generation—all those who might be considered responsible for the plight of the soldiers— and extended to all civilians, including women, to all who could not or at least did not share the soldier's lot.

Owen's extremely strong sense of identification with men who fought and suffered by his side led him to embrace the principle of sharing, participation, and empathy with others as a fundamental part of humanity and, as in "Insensibility," to view ultimate dehumanization as the loss of this capacity. It led him in several other poems to arraign and condemn not only the Church but other specific kinds or groups of persons for their ignorance and indifference. In these poems, which are Owen's most bitter, though not usually his best, his anger and contempt are so strong that occasionally his clear vision blurs and his poetic control wavers. The tone of such poems as "The Dead-Beat," "S.I.W.," or "Smile, Smile, Smile" is far from the grave, impersonal one of "Futility," "Anthem," and "Insensibility." The edge of shrillness suggests a loss of perspective and renders these poems less effective and memorable than those which treat their subject in a less personal manner.

The father of the young soldier who shoots himself in "S.I.W." sends him off to war with "Death sooner than dishonour, that's the style!" The older generation who write the newspaper articles in "Smile, Smile, Smile" repeat the old catchwords of honor and patriotism which fail to conceal their hypocrisy, greed, and utter indifference to the men who have died:

> Peace would do wrong to our undying dead,—
> The sons we offered might regret they died

> If we got nothing lasting in their stead.
> We must be solidly indemnified.

"The Dead-Beat," one of Owen's bitterest poems, describes the utter collapse of a youngster whose will to live has been undermined by the callousness of those at home:

> A low voice said,
> "It's Blighty, p'raps, he sees; his pluck's all gone,
> Dreaming of all the valiant, that aren't dead:
> Bold uncles, smiling ministerially;
> Maybe his brave young wife, getting her fun
> In some new home, improved materially.
> It's not these stiffs have crazed him; nor the Hun."

The end of the poem represents "the Doc," a figure of the older generation of noncombatants, rejoicing over the youngster's death.

The willful disregard of war's realities by those who have not experienced them finds its most successful expression in "Dulce et Decorum Est." This poem was a direct result of Owen's anger at the verses of a newspaper poet, Jessie Pope, which expressed the traditional heroic sentiments so wholly inappropriate to mechanized warfare. Beginning with a grimly realistic dramatization of the fate of a gas casualty—

> If in some smothering dreams you too could pace
> Behind the wagon that we flung him in,
> And watch the white eyes writhing in his face,
> His hanging face, like a devil's sick of sin;
> If you could hear, at every jolt, the blood
> Come gargling from the froth-corrupted lungs,
> Obscene as cancer, bitter as the cud
> Of vile, incurable sores on innocent tongues,—

Owen concludes with a scornful and passionate refutation of: "The old Lie: Dulce et decorum est/Pro patria mori." The poet's indignation and bitterness find in this poem an expression both lofty and cutting.

From the guilt of ignorance and indifference to that of actual responsibility is but a step. Owen's strong feeling that both Christianity and humanity had been betrayed by the powers of Church and State led him once or twice to arraign the Almighty Himself, the supreme symbol of authority, on the capital charge of murder. In "Parable," he used the Old Testament story of the sacrifice of Isaac to declare the guilt of the old, of fathers who murder their sons by sending them to war. In "Soldier's Dream," God Himself, rather than a human father, is the murderer; and the opposition between father and son on the human level finds its counterpart in the opposition between "kind Jesus," who stops the war by damaging all the weapons, and God, who gives plenary power to the militant archangel Michael to repair them.

"Soldier's Dream" is not a good poem, but it is a very interesting one. Like all dreams, it holds in solution a number of themes and attitudes that were part of the movement of Owen's mind. It is a clear and wholly unsophisticated expression of his basic subjects, guilt and sacrifice, his characteristic analogy between the soldier and Christ, and his own sense of identification with both. It shows his feeling of the overt hostility of authority figures toward the soldiers: of old to young, of fathers to sons, of God to Christ. God is not the loving Father of the New Testament but the wrathful Jehovah of the Old; Christ is Son and Sacrifice; the soldier is the son of his father and a sacrifice for his father's sins of pride and lack of pity. Theologically unsound as it may be, Owen's picture of the opposition between Jesus and God is the reflection of the conflict he felt between young men who were dying and those who sent them to die; and his own psychological alienation from his father doubtless made it easier for him to identify with the suffering sons.

"Inspection," a poem on the same subject, is considerably more subtle in treatment and implications. This is a dramatic dialogue between an officer and a soldier found dirty on parade. The dirt, the officer later discovers, is blood: "He told me, afterwards, the damnèd spot/Was blood, his own. 'Well, blood is dirt,' I said." The quotation from *Macbeth* suggests with particular effectiveness the theme of the poem in which blood becomes both the stain of guilt and the means of washing it out:

> "The world is washing out its stains," he said.
> "It doesn't like our cheeks so red:
> Young blood's its great objection.

But when we're duly white-washed, being dead,
The race will bear Field-Marshal God's inspection."

The bloodguilt and the means of purging it are one and the same, the deaths of young soldiers; and this process of purgation is therefore an inverted and negative one. Life, not death, becomes the crime which must be purged, which is unacceptable to God, and He Himself the symbol of those responsible for death. Like black magic, the poem stands religion on its head; writes the Lord's Prayer backward and hangs it upside down, as did witches in the Middle Ages; and makes of God a devil in the uniform of a Field Marshal.

It must be noted at this point that Owen was not always consistent in his attitudes, despite the fact that his war poems in general display a remarkable coherence in themes and viewpoints. This occasional inconsistency is most notable in his treatment of God, as can be seen in a number of poems which exhibit fluctuations in mood and in point of view. He sees God sometimes as judge, sometimes as devil; as indifferent, as tender, as implacable; and sometimes Owen seems to deny and sometimes to hope. He is undecided, in fact, as to exactly what he does think. He is a poet, and a particularly harried young one at that, not a philosopher responsible for developing a logically coherent body of thought.

The sonnet "On Seeing a Piece of Our Artillery Brought into Action" illustrates his indecision, as well as the distance he had traveled poetically since, say, "The One Remains" or "The Fates." Most striking is the poem's implication, an admission Owen nowhere else makes, that war may sometimes be necessary and justified. But, because it blasts innocent and guilty alike, the poet prays, ". . . when thy spell be cast complete and whole/May God curse thee, and cut thee from our soul!" The God who will curse arms when Arrogance has been put down is not the God of "Soldier's Dream," who sends the archangel Michael to repair the arms Jesus has damaged, nor the Field Marshal of "Inspection" who desires the blood of youth, nor even the God in "Exposure" whose love is dying. He is much closer to the Christian God who loves the world, who suffers with those who suffer, and who will at last release the souls of men from the guilt that burdens them. The sonnet not only offers a different view of God, it differs from all the other war poems both in tone and in diction. Instead of the quiet, grave impersonality of "Anthem" or "Futility;" the colloquial, conversational diction and movement of the descriptive pieces, or the irony and anger of the satires, this poem employs a grandly rhetorical vocabulary and syntax, using such archaisms as "thou," "thy," and "yea," and such "poetic" terms as "malison" and "spoilure" without a trace of self-consciousness or a hint of artificiality. It is like a return, on another level entirely, to the typical vocabulary and manner of so much of his juvenilia. But what was grandiose has become grandeur, what was forced and artificial has become true feeling, and what was mannered and rather precious now has the accent of an achieved individuality.

V *Slayer and Slain*

Owen's search for a scapegoat and his readiness to accuse the powers of Church and State and of the universe itself of responsibility for the hell of war represent real and permanent aspects of his general theme of guilt. In his greatest poems—ones neither of realism nor of satire but of imagination and prophecy—what he emphasizes, however, is the involvement of all men in guilt; and his poems become elegies for those who are at one and the same time innocent sacrifices and guilty sinners, slayers and slain. In this more complex, more philosophical view the soldier is not merely sacrificial victim but, through his participation in war and its inevitable effect on his own soul, is as guilty as the Field Marshal.

"Spring Offensive," a poem of imaginative description rather than of prophecy or vision, obtains its effect largely by suggesting what has happened not to those who died but to those who survived. Having entered hell alive and returned in the body, their silence seems to indicate that they feel themselves still in hell, always to live with the knowledge of hell. "Some say God caught them even before they fell," the poet observes of the men who died in battle; but those who have returned from battle alive say nothing. Whether we conclude that their experience of hell has taught them there is no God, or whether, having taken part in hell, they feel themselves sundered forever from the knowledge and love of God, we cannot know for sure. But it is clear that they are silent because, if they spoke, it could only be to say, like Mar-

lowe's Mephistopheles, "Why, this is hell, nor am I out of it."
Those who have entered hell must live forevermore in the knowledge of it.

"Mental Cases," which treats the same theme more explicitly, is
one of Owen's most grimly realistic poems in its images of the
deranged soldiers themselves and its description of the sights that
have deranged them. It is their own sense of guilt that has driven
them mad: "Memory fingers in their hair of murders,/multitudi-
nous murders they once witnessed"; and the blood they have seen
and helped to shed now colors day and night for them. But their
guilt is only part of the total, which includes in a much greater
degree the guilt of the sane, and the gestures of the mad seem to
accuse those responsible:

> —Thus their hands are plucking at each other;
> Picking at the rope-knouts of their scourging;
> Snatching after us who smote them, brother,
> Pawing us who dealt them war and madness.

"You! hypocrite lecteur!—mon semblable,—mon frère!" T. S.
Eliot, echoing Baudelaire, thus brings the reader with him into
the Waste Land. So Owen emphasizes the brotherhood of all men,
if not in love, then in guilt. The poem is particularly poignant
when we recall that the poet himself experienced a nervous, if not
a mental, collapse and underwent fairly prolonged treatment in a
hospital for neurasthenic disorders. In a letter to his cousin, Leslie
Gunston, with whom he had spent a day's leave, Owen wrote that,
as he walked back to his army camp, he "could almost see the
dead lying about in the hollows of the downs." [9] Clearly he is
identified both with the mad soldiers themselves, tortured by
guilt, and also, as his use of the pronoun "us" emphasizes, with the
sane who have helped to drive them mad.

"The Send-Off," one of Owen's lesser known but very successful
poems, is akin to "Spring Offensive" in imaginative and suggestive
power; and the poem haunts the mind with the sense it evokes of
the secret and unacknowledged evil of the world. The troops, who
wear the flowers given them as if they were already dead—a grim
jest the truth of which they are to learn—are seen off to war only
by "dull porters" and "a casual tramp." The inhuman and inexorable machinery which will bring about their actual deaths is im-

plied in the one adjective "unmoved," while "winked" conveys a
hint of conspiracy between the machines and their guardians and
manipulators: "Then, unmoved, signals nodded, and a lamp/
Winked to the guard." The suggestion that the soldiers are victims
of a monstrous conspiracy strengthens with the image of the next
stanza, and the ignorance of those left behind is a token of the
success with which it operates:

> So secretly, like wrongs hushed-up, they went.
> They were not ours:
> We never heard to which front these were sent.

The poem concludes, like "Spring Offensive," with the effect of
war on the few who return:

> A few, a few, too few for drums and yells,
> May creep back, silent, to still village wells
> Up half-known roads.

Like the survivors of "Spring Offensive," they have nothing to say
of their experiences or their comrades; and we are left to wonder
whether their village roads are only half remembered by them
because of the length of their absence or the intensity and terror
of the events in which they have taken part. "The rest is silence."

"The Show" operates on a different level from these poems.
Neither observation nor imagination in the usual sense govern its
details but a kind of hallucinatory and apocalyptic insight which
makes it one of the most terrible poems ever to be written about
war. Owen's revulsion at inhumanity and bestiality is embodied in
the vision of a foul insect world, more nightmarish than the scenes
of Hieronymous Bosch, a world of caterpillars infesting the slimy
and stinking head of a corpse. The head is the landscape of the
Western Front; its beard, the barbed wire; its pockmarks and
scabs of plague, the shellholes; and the swarms of brown and gray
caterpillars that "ramp" upon each other to eat and be eaten, the
troops on both sides. Death is the master of ceremonies of this
show; and, when the poet faints at the horror of the sight spread
out beneath him,

> . . . Death fell with me, like a deepening moan.
> And He, picking a manner of worm, which half had hid

Its bruises in the earth, but crawled no further,
Showed me its feet, the feet of many men,
And the fresh-severed head of it, my head.

Anger, scorn, even horror have given way to a kind of cosmic
disgust; the dehumanization of men by war could hardly be rendered more vividly. In this ghastly business all are implicated, and
by it condemned; but, though the gazer may faint at his awful
vision, he can still look unflinchingly at his own share in universal
guilt.

"Strange Meeting," the poem by which Owen is best known,
gathers up and weaves together with great symbolic and suggestive power his most fundamental themes and attitudes.[10] A soldier
dreams of escaping from battle and meeting face to face in hell
another, whom at the poem's end he learns that he has killed.
"That other" was, like himself, a seeker after beauty and truth—a
poet and prophet who might, had he lived, have offered the world
salvation from its barbarism and bestiality. Now, however, the
hope of the future lies slain, and men face "the undone years,/The
hopelessness" of a world dehumanized by the violence of war.

The dreamer has descended into his unconscious to confront his
own inner self, both enemy and alter ego, whom as a soldier he
has slain. In killing his "enemy" he has killed a man like himself;
his own best self; and the better part of men unborn who will now
be less than wholly human in the absence of the salvation the
dreamer might have offered them had he kept his spirit untainted
by hate and aggression. The unmistakable allusion to the Agony
in the Garden suggests that the dreamer, by taking part in the
bloodshed, has slain his own hope of redemption, the Christ
within himself, as well as the hope of the world:

I would have poured my spirit without stint
But not through wounds; not on the cess of war.
Foreheads of men have bled where no wounds were.

By participating in war he has lost the spirit of pity, the sense of
empathy and identification with all men, the one hope for the
regeneration of the individual and of mankind. Physical death is
thus the symbol of the spiritual death both of the person and of
society. "I am the enemy you killed, my friend," echoes with pro-

found poignance Dylan Thomas's statement, "There is only one war, that of men against men." [11]

More, perhaps, than any other of Owen's poems, "Strange Meeting" reaches out beyond personality and particular time and place to embrace all men and all wars. The dreamer escapes from the battle in which he is involved.

> Down some profound dull tunnel, long since scooped
> Through granites which titanic wars had groined.
> Yet also there encumbered sleepers groaned,

The past, "long since" over, with its own titanic wars and their guilt under which men groan, is part of the dreamer's vision, and his own sense of guilt is part of an age-old iniquity. His vision of the future suggests the continuance of war and its evil: the years to come are undone through the inexorable working of cause and effect, the impact of war on the souls of men. The primal curse of Cain is handed down from one generation to another; and all men, past, present, and future, are involved in and destroyed by it. Slain and slayers alike are victims; and the poem, like others of Owen, is an elegy not so much for the dead as for the living of the present and the future. Human brotherhood, universal guilt, Owen's own personal sense of guilt—the "very seared conscience" of which he wrote Osbert Sitwell—the identification of the slain soldier with Christ, the role of the poet as prophet, spokesman for and savior of humanity, salvation through pity, the dehumanization of individual and of society by war: all come together in the pattern of this poem.

VI   *The Subject Is War*

"My subject is War and the pity of War." It is now possible to understand more clearly the meaning of that seemingly simple statement, and to be astonished ever anew at the difference between Owen's early verse—or the verse of whatever date in which he reverts to his earlier manner—and the great poems of his maturity. The lushness and the prettiness, the self-absorption and the mannerisms, the artificialities of emotion and of diction, the dreams of love and of fame—all have been cleansed as by fire. To the treatment of his tragic view of man's fate, Owen brought the poetic power he had been developing and a moral power he had never shown before. His great poems are not simply better than the early verses; they are different in kind. So true to fact and to feeling are they, so unswervingly honest in their presentation of fact, so impersonal and controlled in their emotion, that some commentators have mistaken their strength for "Godlike detachment," or complained of their "passivity." [12] Rhetoric and false feeling are so rare in them that, when they do make a momentary appearance, as in Owen's treatment of noncombatants or his accusations against the old, they are the more jarring by contrast. His best poems are characterized by harsh realism in combination with imaginative power and a deeply religious attitude, by fervent feeling held in strict control, by objectivity and impersonality leagued with an extraordinary power of identification and empathy.

The catalyst of war precipitated this poetry, after the long, slow years during which Owen was preparing for his poethood. Both were necessary; neither, alone, would have sufficed. The war did not make Owen a poet; but it enabled him finally to make poetry. In it he found a subject which focused all the powers of his mind and soul on one purpose. The exigencies of his situation and the brevity of his life afforded him no time to explore other subjects, to which he might have brought the same honesty, the same passion, and the same lofty vision.

Sir Henry Newbolt's complaint, in his letter to Sassoon quoted above, that Owen's poems were "almost all on one note," however, is unjust. Within the limits of his subject and his prevailing mood of pity, understood in its larger tragic context, it is surprising how different all his poems are from one another. Each explores a different aspect or reveals a different implication of the general subject; the tone varies from seemingly dispassionate to bitterly ironic to elegiac; the viewpoint is now intensely personal, and again dramatic and objective; the perspective ranges from close-up to telescopic; the lyric of immediate personal response gives way to the poem of dramatic description, and it in turn to poems of imaginative or visionary character. Here, the diction is terse, colloquial, conversational; there, grandly rhetorical; once or twice, even, the poet writes in dialect; the grimmest concrete realism of word or image shoulders an august abstraction worthy of Sophocles or Shakespeare. Unity there is, certainly, but it is unity amid abundant variety.

Poetry is more than its subject or the attitudes and emotions generated by its themes. Owen's poetry, like all poetry, ultimately succeeds or fails by virtue of his executive ability to convert his vision into language—to find and combine the word, the image, the rhythm which will both re-create and communicate what he sees and feels. His earlier poetry is often technically accomplished and reveals his interest in experiment and his care for craftsmanship. But, except in flashes here and there, it does not prepare the reader for the skill which, in his mature poetry, he exhibits in transcribing reality of fact and feeling into words, for the power and precision of his diction, the individual quality of phrasing and rhythm, the striking and unique imagery. In his best poems, form and content are one; and the voice his own and none other. His early experiments with sound and movement often seemed to be independent of the inner life of the poem, unrelated to meaning or emotion. Now all his technical skill is at the service of imagination and feeling. His poetry is not only war and the pity of war but craftsmanship, and it is this craft that must now be examined.

CHAPTER 4

My Craft or Art

DESPITE Wilfred Owen's rejection of "Poetry," he was from the beginning and remained always a very conscious craftsman. His latest editor, C. Day Lewis, has pointed out how increasingly self-critical he became as time went on: "If we follow the successive drafts of the poems over which he worked longest—'Anthem for Doomed Youth,' for instance—we can see how admirably he kept sharpening the language, focusing ever more clearly his theme." [1] Owen's feeling for form, for verbal precision, and for the musical value of words are among his chief attributes as a poet; and his instinct for craftsmanship is indeed the main link between his juvenile verse and the war poems of his maturity.

Owen's verbal sense, as much as his sensuousness, explains the influence of Keats; and his youthful poetry shows his delight in open vowel sounds, in rich and fluid feminine endings, and in alliteration. His early and continuing care for the sound and shape of words; for the careful choice of the exact verb, adjective, or adverb; for the balance of phrase and clause; and for movement and rhythm counteracts the overlushness of much of his juvenilia as later it controlled the bitterness, the anger, or the despair of his war poetry. Especially was he concerned and constantly experimenting with sound patterns. More than most poetry Owen's is addressed to the ear and should be read aloud for its full effect. It is his remarkable gift for sounds and his experiments with auditory devices that has attracted most critical attention and constitutes his chief claim as an innovator of new forms and a renovator of English poetic idiom.

Sound devices, assonances and dissonances, are of course common in all good poetry. It is not the mere presence of these effects but Owen's special use of them which is arresting, particularly in his later poems. His early verse testifies to his musical ear and to his interest in experimenting with sound, but it reveals nothing that was not the common property of all his predecessors. His devices such as alliteration tend to be decorative rather than structural in function. They exist individually, without cross-references and echoes, without vital relationships to the emotional content and the life of the poem as a whole. The war poems, existing as they do on a different level of poetic and moral power, exhibit also a different and far more complex and controlled use of auditory patterns. Assonance, alliteration, and half-rhyme, Owen's particular hallmark, are now an inseparable part of mood and meaning, of cadence and movement; and the sound effects no longer merely please the ear but contribute tellingly to the poem's final impact. His is a poetry of verbal resonance and echo, rich in varying vowel and consonant combinations, with strong internal patterning as well as consonantal end-rhyme.

I *Half-rhyme*

Half-rhyme was not Owen's invention, but because he used it more systematically and strikingly than any poet before him—or after, for that matter—it was from the beginning the feature of his verse that most struck commentators; and it has come to be peculiarly associated with him. Half-rhyme, known also as para-rhyme, vowel dissonance, or consonantal end-rhyme, is simple in principle. Instead of keeping the vowel sound and changing the consonant, as true rhyme does (*mud/blood*), it keeps the consonant sound and changes the vowel (*feet/fought, selves/solves*). Its first use in Owen's poetry, as yet tentative and undeveloped, is in the slight but charming fragment "From My Diary, July 1914" which, unlike so many of Owen's poems, can thus be dated with certainty. He continued to experiment with half-rhyme and used it extensively in his later poetry. Where he found the suggestion for this technique has been a matter of question, but the answer now seems fairly certain.[2]

Before Owen, this device had been used by at least three poets writing in English: Henry Vaughan in the seventeenth century and Emily Dickinson and Gerard Manley Hopkins in the nineteenth. It seems unlikely, however, that Owen knew the work of any of them. Dickinson, though she had been published in England, was not at all well known at that time; most of Hopkins was as yet unpublished; and there is no evidence to suggest Owen's acquaintance with Vaughan. As we have already seen, Owen's reading of poetry had been chiefly the nineteenth-century Romantics and the Georgians who followed. These are well represented in the small library he left at his death, while none of the three poets in question appears.

Another possible source from which he might have derived the suggestion for half-rhyme is Welsh poetry, the source used by Vaughan and Hopkins. Cynghanedd, an elaborate patterning of internal rhyme, alliteration, and assonance, had been an element of Welsh versification for centuries. Robert Graves, a contemporary and friend of Owen's, himself had borrowed some of the metrical devices of Welsh poetry for his own verse. But Graves has never suggested that he had any influence on Owen's poetry; and, despite Welsh attempts to claim him as a countryman, Owen knew no Welsh. It does not seem probable that he found here the suggestion for half-rhyme.

A much stronger case can be made for French verse and that of Jules Romains in particular as the direct influence on Owen, not merely in regard to half-rhyme itself but in his experiments with sound patterns in general. That Owen knew Romains' work must be reckoned virtually certain, despite the fact that, like Vaughan, Dickinson, and Hopkins, Romains is not represented among his books. Owen had studied French for years, read and spoke it with ease, and wrote it well enough to be complimented by his elderly friend Laurent Tailhade on his feeling for nuance and idiom. Tailhade, himself a poet, who took a deep interest in Owen and his verse, may have known Romains personally. That he introduced the young man to Romains' verse is very likely. During his residence in Bordeaux Owen had every opportunity for acquainting himself with French poetry, including that of his contemporaries. Romains had already (in 1908) published one volume of poems, *La Vie Unanime,* and in 1913, the year Owen went to France, his second, *Odes et Prières,* appeared. Both these volumes put into practice Romains' poetic theories, and especially his use of *accords,* as he terms his various experiments with rhyme and assonance. It seems altogether likely that the young Englishman with his musical ear, his interest in sound effects, and his affinity for French would have been attracted by both theory and practice.

The theory behind Romains' verses was later (in 1923) formulated in his *Petit Traité de Versification*. A glance at some of his classifications of technique shows how close to them are many of Owen's characteristic effects of rhyme and assonance. Romains' *rime imparfaite*, for example (multit*ude*/amert*ume*), is Owen's half-rhyme; Romains' *rime renversée* in which homophony—likeness or identity—of the vowel is accompanied by inversion of the adjacent consonants (ju*lep*/archi*pel*) has many analogues in Owen's verse (*saw*/*wa*tched, t*rembles*/*limbs*); Romains' juggling of the position of the rhyme in successive lines, the rhyme word occurring now initially, now in the interior of the line, now at the end, is paralleled in many instances in Owen's poems; and *rime par augmentation* (amor*ti*/dome*stique*) and *rime par diminution* (é*toiles*/*toits*) also occurs in Owen. What Romains held essential was a harmonious progression achieved by varying vowel and consonant combinations—"systems of sonorities" as he called them—and these symphonic sound effects are so striking a feature of Owen's poetry as to compel the conclusion that, at the very least, he was strongly influenced by Romains' experiments.

II *Early Experiments*

"From My Diary" is clearly a transitional poem, both in technique and in content. Akin to much of Owen's early verse in its sensuous Keatsian echoes, the last half-dozen lines in particular are reminiscent of the odes to Psyche and to Melancholy; and it combines some stock themes of the early verse—Nature, Poetry, and Love. On the other hand, its details are closer to real, observed nature than is quite usual in Owen's juvenilia; and the suggestion of personal experience in such a line as "Wakening with wonder in the Pyrenees" is a new note. The real world is beginning to break in on the world of dreams.

The most immediately striking feature of its technique is the short line of only one or two syllables which precedes each longer, conventionally rhyming line and furnishes a counterpoint of half-rhyme to the regular chime of the couplet:

> Leaves
>   Murmuring by myriads in the shimmering trees.
> Lives
>   Wakening with wonder in the Pyrenees.

Birds
Cheerily chirping in the early day.
Bards
Singing of summer, scything thro' the hay.

The poet thus combines conventional true rhyme with his first tentative use of half-rhyme, groping for a handhold on his new tool, not yet at all sure what he could do with it. The half-rhymes remain semi-detached from the body of the poem itself, contributing to its effect but as yet ornamental, a plaything, not a device intrinsic to mood or meaning. Not so immediately obvious, but full of promise for the future, is the use of assonance within the line. This is not, as at first sight it might seem, a mere matter of alliteration. There is a subtle repetition and half-rhyme of syllables within the line, a melodic undertone running from line to line against the heavy beat of the short half-rhyme line: "*Murmur*ing by *myr*iads in the *shimmer*ing trees," "*Cheer*ily *chir*ping in the *ear*ly day," "*Bur*sting the *sur*face of the *ebony* pond." A line like "Of swimmers *carv*ing thro' the *spar*kling cold" exhibits Owen's use of Romains' *rime renversée*, the hard *k* sound continued with "cold," and re-emphasized in the voiced *g* consonant of the next line, "*Gl*eaming with wetness to the morning *gold*." The vowels of the alliterated syllables show Owen's characteristic progression from a vowel of high to one of low pitch, a technique first noticed by Michael Roberts;[3] but it is not as yet systematically exploited for its emotional effect. Later, in the war poems, Owen used it with great skill to produce a sensation of frustration, weariness, or hopelessness, directly reinforcing with this auditory device the general effect at which he aimed. "From My Diary" is fragmentary and halting by comparison with later poems, yet it points unmistakably toward the development of a virtuoso handling of verbal melody.

"Exposure," written in February, 1917, nearly three years later than "From My Diary," is the next instance of Owen's use of half-rhyme which can be dated with certainty. Though there is no manuscript evidence for other experiments with this technique between the two poems, the evidence is plain to read within the poem itself. The poet is no longer testing his new device; he is using it for his purpose with an assurance that must have been developed with much practice. At the same time, the sound patterns of "Exposure" are a trifle obtrusive and overemphatic beside those of such late poems as "Insensibility" and "Futility" in which they are integrated into the pattern and total effect with great subtlety.

"Exposure" is written in five-line stanzas, four long lines of thirteen or fourteen syllables rounded off by a short fifth line of five or six syllables. The effect is that of a quatrain in an *abba* pattern of half-rhymes, with a coda or tailpiece, unrhymed, commenting on and summing up the effect of the stanza. The irregular, spasmodic effect which is so striking a feature of the poem is attained partly through the use of the half-rhymes and partly by the juxtaposition of the long and short lines, by a profusion of feminine endings, and by irregularity in the frequency and position of stresses within the line. Verbally and kinesthetically the poem is full of tension and discordance, esthetic equivalents of subject and mood. One or two stanzas illustrate the poet's complex use of assonance as well as half-rhyme and show how much he had developed these verbal tools since "From My Diary":

> Our brains ache, in the merciless iced east winds that knive
> us . . .
> Wearied, we keep awake because the night is silent . . .
> Low, drooping flares confuse our memory of the salient . . .
> Worried by silence, sentries whisper, curious, nervous,
>   But nothing happens.

The short, slow, emphatic first phrase with its long *a* sounds passes at once into the long but much swifter second phrase, with its variation of long and short *i*'s, the onomatopoeic hissing of the *s*'s to emphasize the east wind, and the dissonance of the *iced/east* half-rhyme. The second line repeats the emphasis of the first phrase in its strong opening stress, echoes *ache* with the true rhyme of *awake* within the line (a device recommended by Romains), and emphasizes the long *i* sound of the first line in *night* and *silent*. The *s* sound is picked up in the third line and echoed no less than seven times in the fourth, the whispering of the "curious, nervous" sentries made manifest. *Worried* adds half-rhyme here at the beginning as well as at the end of the line, chiming with *wearied* both in sound and sense; *silence* echoes *silent*, reinforcing with repetition almost but not quite identical after the half-rhyme of *salient; nervous* completes the quatrain with a daring but successful half-rhyme; and the short, unrhymed fifth line adds its note of frustration and inconsequence.

> Watching, we hear the mad gusts tugging on the wire,
> Like twitching agonies of men among its brambles.
> Northward, incessantly, the flickering gunnery rumbles,
> Far off, like a dull rumour of some other war.
>   What are we doing here?

The second stanza opens with another emphatic stress, repeating the *w* of *wearied* and *worried,* but with a vowel pitched low in Owen's typical falling cadence, a progression of vowel sounds which here seem to suggest the gamut of painful sensations ranging from acute tension and fatigue to boredom and numbness: *wea*ried/*wo*rried/*wa*tching. *Gusts* is followed immediately by the inverted echo of *tug*ging, and repeated in the second and third lines with a*go*nies and *gun*nery, while the triple *ing* chime of the participle seems to anchor us in a timeless present, an effect reinforced by the echo of the half-rhyme in *twitching,* paired with *watching.* And beneath the thud of the hard *g*'s and the duller thump of the short *u*'s is the vibrating nasal of *n*'s and *m*'s with their short vowels: a*go*nies/*men*/a*mong*/b*ram*bles/*gun*nery/*rum*-bles/*rum*our/*some,* like a plucked string humming, or the wind on the barbed wire. The stanzas of the poem are knit together by this skillful interplay of vowel and consonant sounds, and the half-rhymes accord perfectly with the nervous, jerky, irregularly stressed phrases. It is a poetry of relationships and cross-references of sound, full of echoes and anticipations, in which sound and movement become as important as meaning, become one with meaning.

"Exposure" also illustrates what was to become one of Owen's most characteristic treatments of consonant clusters. Alliterative elements in his verse sometimes consist of a single phonetic element repeated, either in couples, thus, "as we slashed *b*ones *b*are/ Not to feel sickness or re*m*orse of *m*urder"; or in a longer sequence, "*S*udden *s*ucce*ss*ive flights of bullet*s s*treak the *s*ilence." Oftener, they consist of compounds: "With sidelong *fl*owing *fl*akes that *fl*ock, pause, and renew." These latter have been dubbed "circumsyllabic sequences" by David Masson and defined as "a discernible succession of members, each of which consists of two or more sound-components in the same order in each member."[4] Owen developed a technique of varying the interval between the components, a tight compound loosening or a loose one tightening as the line progressed. An example of the former is the first line of "Exposure"'s fourth stanza: "Pale *fl*akes with fingering stealth come *f*eeling for our faces—," where the tightly linked *fl* of *fl*akes has loosened in *f*eeling. An example of the latter, in which the interval tightens from a looser one, is: "And gave their *l*aughs more g*l*ee. . . ." Such phonetic patterns are a recurring element in Owen's later poems, but they are almost never simple in effect or easy to disentangle from other consonant and vowel designs around them. These richly interwoven sound patterns at their best furnish a music which is compelling without being obtrusive, which binds together and provides continuity between phrases and lines, and which reinforces mood and meaning.

III   *Sound and Rhythm*

After "Exposure," early in 1917, Owen experimented constantly with the resources of sound and rhythm. All his mature poems reveal, to some extent, his careful shaping of music and movement. His sound effects vary from the simple onomatopoeia of lines like "And thud! flump! thud! down the steep steps came thumping/And sploshing in the flood, deluging muck—/The sentry's body" or "Machine-guns chuckled,—Tut-tut! Tut-tut!" or "Only the stuttering rifles' rapid rattle," to the complex, symphonic effects of "Insensibility"; from the quiet melody of vowel cadences to the percussion of consonant combinations; and in his great poems they are inseparable from the poem's total meaning. The effect of his poems depends almost equally on his skillful manipulation of rhythm. The breaking of the five-line stanza of "The Send-Off" into three- and two-line groups by its slowing of the movement has the effect of universalizing the fate of the departing troops, so that we regard the scene not as one episode of a particular war but under the aspect of eternity. In "Spring Offensive" when the soldiers turn from peaceful meditation to battle, the verse races with them, quickening from the slow, sensuous melody of the first three stanzas into the alarm of the fourth and the fury of the fifth:

> So soon they topped the hill, and raced together
> Over an open stretch of herb and heather
> Exposed. And instantly the whole sky burned
> With fury against them; earth set sudden cups
> In thousands for their blood; and the green slope
> Chasmed and steepened sheer to infinite space.

In "Mental Cases," the confusion and pain of the mad soldiers are suggested by the inversion of word order and the short, abrupt phrases: "Who are these? Why sit they here in twilight?/Wherefore rock they, purgatorial shadows?" The dramatic realism of "S.I.W." gives way in the third section, called "The Poem," to a lyric passage re-creating the state of mind that brought the young soldier to shoot himself:

> It was the reasoned crisis of his soul
> Against more days of inescapable thrall,
> Against infrangibly wired and blind trench wall
> Curtained with fire, roofed in with creeping fire,
> Slow grazing fire, that would not burn him whole
> But kept him for death's promises and scoff,
> And life's half-promising, and both their riling.

Here not only do the tone and diction heighten from the colloquial, conversational, realistic level of the rest of the poem, but the movement of the verse becomes stately and dignified, and the repetition of word and phrase, particularly in lines 4 and 5, creates a sense of the intolerable psychological pressures that caused the soldier's suicide. In much the same way, "Inspection" passes from the crisp dialogue of the first section to the ironic but more lyrical commentary of the second. The total impact of Owen's war poems thus depends directly on the verbal and rhythmic patterns of the verse. The varied effects he achieved can be illustrated more fully in a closer examination of three or four of his most successful poems.

"Arms and the Boy," apparently one of the last half-dozen poems Owen wrote (July, 1918), is particularly notable for the tight precision and control of its structure, diction, and verbal patterns. Its brief twelve lines are arranged in three stanzas of four lines each, the lines paired by their half-rhymes. The movement of the first two stanzas is slow and deliberate, the tone calm and apparently impersonal, almost cold. The diction, hard, concrete, yet highly connotative, accords with movement and tone. But the verbal patterns the poet sets up tell a different story, contrasting with the apparent objectivity of his attitude. In the first two stanzas vowel and consonant combinations convey an indescribably sinister and malignant impression, with a succession of thudding stopped consonants, *s*'s thickening into *sh*'s and fully voiced *z*'s, and irregular half-rhymes occurring within the line as well as at the end.

> Let the boy try along this bayonet-blade
> How cold steel is, and keen with hunger of blood;
> Blue with all malice, like a madman's flash;
> And thinly drawn with famishing for flesh.

The half-rhyme of *boy* and *bay* is interrupted by the syllable *try*, akin in sound to both and linking them in a drawn-out sequence which continues with *blade*. *Blade* adds the *l* sound to the repetition of *b*, repeats the long *a* of *bay*, and ends the line with the heavy *d*. *L* and *d* are picked up in the *cold* of the second line; *l* is repeated in *steel*, and its long *e* is echoed with the vowel rhyme of *keen*, which also repeats the hard *k* consonant of *cold*. *Hunger* reinforces the *k* sound with its voiced *g*, and *blade*'s half-rhyme *blood* ends the line, its *lod* combination harmonizing with the *old* of *cold*, and exhibiting a variation of Romains' *rime renversée*. Here in two lines are no fewer than eight half-rhymes of different vowel and consonant combinations, the dominant sound that of the heavy voiced consonants and the long vowels.

The next line repeats the *bl* combination and the *l* sound is now released from its consonants and paired with vowels in the *all/al/li/li/la* sequence of "all malice, like a madman's flash." *Flash* is paired with its half-rhyme *flesh*, and the last line thickens in sound with the *sh*'s of *famishing* and *flesh* and the *th* of *thinly*. The second stanza continues these sound effects with the "*blind, blunt bullet-leads*"; *nuzzle* and *zinc* emphasize the *s*'s with their voiced *z* sound; and *teeth, sharp, sharpness,* and *death* underline the *sh*'s and *th*'s of the first stanza. Both stanzas are heavy and clotted with the menace conveyed by these verbal effects. In the third stanza when the poem turns from the malignant weapons of war to the image of innocence and youth, the movement of the verse

quickens and a succession of rippling *s*'s and *l*'s make the hitherto
thick, heavy line light and flexible.

"Insensibility" at first sight seems irregular and loosely struc-
tured beside the tight precision of "Arms and the Boy." Its six
stanzas range in length from seven to twelve lines each, and the
lines themselves vary from four to eleven syllables in length. Half-
rhymes occur at irregular intervals, sometimes forming a couplet,
sometimes skipping four or five lines to pick up their matching
sound in a different syntactical context. This irregularity of stanza
and line length and rhyme placement is compounded by the irregularity in frequency and placement of the stresses and the variation in movement of the lines, some light and rapid, others slow
and heavy. The total effect is of a kind of casual tone and almost
jerky movement, an impression strengthened by the predomi-
nance of feminine endings. But the looseness and irregularity are
more apparent than real. Again, the subtle but strong verbal patterns function both structurally and rhetorically to bind the poem
into a free-flowing continuum of sound, meaning, and mood. A
stanza or two will illustrate how Owen uses these patterns:

> Happy are men who yet before they are killed
> Can let their veins run cold.
> Whom no compassion fleers
> Or makes their feet
> Sore on the alleys cobbled with their brothers.
> The front line withers,
> But they are troops who fade, not flowers
> For poets' tearful fooling:
> Men, gaps for filling:
> Losses, who might have fought
> Longer; but no one bothers.

The rapid, tripping movement of the long first line, with its succession of short, open, unstressed vowels, modulates into the
much slower second line with its long vowels and strong stresses,
and the slow, deliberate tempo continues through the next two
lines. It quickens again in the long fifth line, slows abruptly in the
sixth, picks up somewhat in the seventh, and again subsides into
the slow, repetitive movement of the last four lines. This variation in pace functions as a rhetorical and dramatic device, reinforcing the impression of a man thinking out loud, following the

turns and twists of his thought as it passes through his mind. Like
the irregularities of the half-rhyme, the movement helps to impart
a kind of spontaneous, almost inconsequential tone to the reflections he is voicing. Counterpointed against this is the verbal music
of an intricate alliteration and assonance, which smooths out the
irregularities of movement and binds lines and stanzas with a running melody.

In this first stanza the dominant sound patterns are the nasals,
m's and *n*'s, and the *f*/*l* combinations. The consonant patterns of
the end-rhymes echo from line to line, chiming not only with their
rhyme-mates but with consonant clusters of other end-rhymes and
with alliterative elements within the line. The hard *k* of *killed* is
repeated in *can*, in its half-rhyme *cold*, in *compassion* and in *cob-
bled*, the last word combining it with the *ld* of the two end-
rhymes. *Fleers* alliterates with *feet*, though its rhyme-mate is not
introduced for three more lines in *flowers*, while the second syllable of *flowers* repeats that of *brothers* and *withers*, close enough
themselves to be reckoned as half-rhyme, though the true rhyme-
mate of *brothers* is *bothers* at the end of the stanza, which furnishes another repetition of the *ers* syllable. The *ers* syllable half-
rhymes with the sequence *Or*/*Sore*/*For* which begin, respectively,
lines 4, 5, and 8, and which furnish a triple true rhyme to contrast
with the half-rhymes. *Fought* in the penultimate line is the mate
of *feet* in the fourth, and the last of a long series of *f*'s of which the
most notable sequence is the *flo*/*for*/*ful*/*fool*/*fill* of lines 7 to 9.

The stanzas themselves are linked by end-rhyme: *feeling* in the
first line of the second stanza recalls the *fooling* and *filling* of the
first, and the second syllable is taken up into another half-rhyme
in *shelling* and *shilling*, the latter a true rhyme with *filling*. *Deci-
mation*, the last word of the second stanza, is repeated in the half-
rhymes of *imagination* and *ammunition* in the first and second
lines of the third stanza, then dropped until the first line of the
fourth stanza where it is repeated with a vowel variation, *notion*.
Pack and *ache*, the second pair of half-rhymes in the third stanza,
are linked to *arithmetic* in the second stanza, until then a loner,
and repeated in the *attack* of the fourth stanza. *Besmirch* and *task*
in the first and third lines of the fifth stanza are half-rhymes for
march and *dusk* in the fourth, and the *march*/*besmirch* sequence
is followed by the repeated echo of *much*: "Alive, he is not vital
over*much*;/ Dying, not mortal over*much*."

In the sixth and final stanza these run-on sound links with preceding stanzas are notably absent, their absence a verbal cue to
the poem's sudden turn and change of mood from melancholy to
indignation, from meditation and reflection to the energetic an-
nouncement of conviction and judgment:

> But cursed are dullards whom no cannon stuns,
> That they should be as stones;
> Wretched are they, and mean
> With paucity that never was simplicity.
> By choice they made themselves immune
> To pity and whatever mourns in man
> Before the last sea and the hapless stars;
> Whatever mourns when many leave these shores;
> Whatever shares
> The eternal reciprocity of tears.

The *k–st* of *cursed* is repeated with a greater interval in *cannon
stuns*, the *st* repeated once more in the half-rhyme *stones*, and the
harsh spitting of the curse is counterpointed and reinforced by the
ominous dull reverberation of the short *u*'s and nasals: d*u*llards/
wh*o*m/*no*/*cannon*/*stuns*/*stones*. The next line introduces the
dominant *m* and *m–n* sequence: *mean*/*simplicity*/*made*/*them*/
immune/*mourns*/*man*/*mourns*/*many*, while the *ch* of *wretched is*
echoed in the strong stress of *choice,* the heaviest syllable in the
stanza. The poem's most poignant line, "Before the last sea and
the hapless stars" repeats the hissing *st* of the first two lines of the
stanza, but is here combined with the long-drawn-out vowels of
last, hap, and st*ars*, while *stars* has as its half-rhyme *tears,* where
the *s* is dropped and the sound echoes the preceding *eternal.* The
whole verbal effect here is no longer energetic and indignant but
unutterably melancholy, all passion spent.

"Futility," a late poem (June, 1918) and one of Owen's finest, is
remarkable for the subtlety of verbal patterns which reflect the
muted, minor key of tone and mood. Its effects are achieved not
by the strong sounds of consonant clusters and combinations but
by the less obtrusive melody of vowel cadences, by rhythm, and
by utter simplicity of diction. Of its brief ninety-one words, sev-
enty-seven are monosyllables. The regular rhyme patterns of the
stanzas mingle true and half-rhyme, and are given additional
prominence by the comparative absence of the cross-references

of sound which are so prominent a feature of other poems. Each stanza is rhymed *ababccc*, but the first and third *c*'s are true rhyme, while the second half-rhymes with them: *snow/now/know*. The progression of short vowels contributes a quiet music of its own, key lines like the first, "Move him into the sun," the last of Stanza 1, "The kind old sun will know," and the first of Stanza 2, "Think how it wakes the seeds," exhibiting Owen's typical falling cadence, a movement from a vowel of higher to one of lower pitch. In the last line, "To break earth's sleep at all," the vowels lengthen and level out, bringing meaning and movement to a gentle but final conclusion.

Rhythm combines with vowel length and pitch and with syntax for emotional effect. The first stanza is comparatively rapid and regular in stress, and the phrases grammatically complex, the meaning running on from line to line. In the second the tone rises, the vowels lengthen, and the rhythm is slowed by a succession of halting adjectival phrases: "Are limbs, so dear-achieved, are sides/ Full-nerved—still warm—too hard to stir?" It is largely this halting and slowing of the movement that gives the next line its tremendous power: "Was it for this the clay grew tall?" Beginning with quiet reflection and expostulation, the poem passes into passionate protest and then dies away with the weary disgust of the last two lines: "O what made fatuous sunbeams toil/To break earth's sleep at all?" No less than "Exposure," "Arms and the Boy," and "Insensibility," "Futility" achieves its effects verbally, but in a manner more subtle and sophisticated, in keeping with the theme and tone of the poem.

Owen was not always so successful in handling his powerful but potentially dangerous techniques. "Strange Meeting," his best-known and in some ways most impressive poem, is weakened by the obtrusiveness of its sound devices in some lines and by an occasional choice of words which seems clever and tricky rather than inevitable. Its opening is arresting and effective:

> It seemed that out of battle I escaped
> Down some profound dull tunnel, long since scooped
> Through granites which Titanic wars had groined . . .

The second line in particular, with its succession of reverberating vowel sounds—*ow/om/o/oun/ul/un/el/ong/oo*—reinforces the sense, and continues with the sequence *ou/an/an/ar/oin* of the third line, booming in the ears like the echoes of a cave. Owen's great predecessors, Donne and Milton, loved such effects: "All whom war, dearth, age, agues, tyrannies/Despair, law, chance hath slain . . . ," and "Avenge, O Lord, Thy slaughtered saints, whose bones/Lie scattered on the Alpine mountains cold," are lines to which Owen's are not unworthy successors. An even more onomatopoeic line is the thirteenth: "And no guns thumped, or down the flues made moan." But the famous couplet, "Courage was mine, and I had mystery,/Wisdom was mine, and I had mastery," is not, in point of fact, very good. Both parallelism and alliteration are too pat, too intrusive, and the pairing of courage with mystery, wisdom with mastery, is sufficiently arbitrary as to excuse even the sympathetic reader for wondering why the choice was made.

Lines like this sound as if Owen were parodying himself, as some of Swinburne's do—"Time with a gift of tears/Grief with a glass that ran"—lines which have moved some who cannot be called Philistines to object that logic would seem rather to assign Time the hourglass and Grief the tears. Such words as "distressful," "richlier," and "trek" weaken rather than strengthen the lines in which they occur and mar the effect of the whole. In "Strange Meeting," too, the half-rhymes are not handled with the skill Owen brought to other poems. They tend to be exclusively paired in couplets instead of echoing from line to line, and their regular recurrence distracts from rather than accentuates mood and theme. "Strange Meeting" is a great poem by virtue of its vision; it owes less to verbal devices than do most of Owen's other war poems.

IV *Convention and Tradition*

Curiously enough, Owen seems to have had little interest in experimenting with a variety of meters or stanza forms. He was not at all the innovator he showed himself in his development and use of half-rhyme and in his exploitation of the possibilities of assonance. He had little of the urge which possesses most young poets to imitate the metrical forms of the past, and his early verse in particular is all extremely conventional in form.

The traditional pattern which most interested him was the sonnet, and in this form he attained great skill, achieving such different effects as the rhetorical grandeur of "The End," or "Sonnet: On Seeing a Piece of Our Artillery Brought into Action," the elegiac lamentation of "Anthem for Doomed Youth," or the unsophisticated candor of that youthful piece of self-revelation, "Maundy Thursday." Only four times did he write conventional blank verse, in "Long Ages Past," "Antaeus: A Fragment," "The Parable of the Old Man and the Young," and "Mental Cases," and of these only two are war poems. In most of his verse he employed a traditional line of eight or ten syllables in iambic meter, though in his later poetry he tended to substitute trochaic or dactylic feet and to place stresses so irregularly that the iambic rhythm is obscured.

Much even of his later war poetry employs full rhyme instead of half, and the rhyme patterns (even when half-rhyme is used) are often couplets or such unremarkable stanza arrangements as the *abab* of "Apologia Pro Poemate Meo," the *aabbba* of "Greater Love," or the *abaab* of "The Send-Off," all of which, incidentally, employ full rhymes. In only fourteen poems did he use half-rhyme, and of these thirteen were written in the last twenty months of his life. Had he lived, it seems reasonable to assume he would have perfected his mastery of half-rhyme and of his other verbal devices, integrating them fully with content and tone as he does in "Futility," and he might have devised as well less conventional metrical patterns in which to employ them. But he died while his poetic powers were still developing, and the verse which he left is as traditional metrically as it is experimental verbally.

V *Vocabulary and Diction*

Sound and rhythm, important as they are in Owen's verse, are not the whole of his poetic characteristics nor the only ones worth remarking. Nothing is more arresting than the difference between the typical diction of his juvenilia and that of his greatest poems. It is true that to the end of his life he retained a weakness for the overlush word and phrase, and he was apt to revert even late in his career to his earlier, conventionally "romantic," sensuous vocabulary. Late poems like "The Kind Ghosts," "Winter Song," and "Song of Songs," as we have already seen, show how strong in him was the temptation to produce verse indistinguishable from that of dozens of late Romantics and Georgians. He was himself well aware of this likeness, and acknowledged Sassoon's help in criti-

cizing some of his pieces and helping him to rid them of this overripe quality, the purple passages that were his inheritance from
Keats and the whole nineteenth-century Romantic tradition.

The experience of reality which shocked him from his dreams
and made him reject "Poetry" made him also find and fashion for
his own uses a vocabulary with which he could tell the truth about
war. Its impact may be seen in the letters in which he tried to
describe for his mother the face of "No Man's Land." So, in his
poems about war, not Beauty but Truth began to dictate. No one
who has read them is likely to forget the concrete realism of word
and image in poems like "Dulce et Decorum Est," "The Sentry,"
"Mental Cases," or "S.I.W." It was such poems as these that
prompted at least the first part of Yeats's famous gibe that "he is
all mud, blood, and sucked sugar-stick" and that also led some
early reviewers to emphasize his realism at the neglect of other,
rarer gifts.

Certainly the realism is there. It is attained partly by his exact
perception of the object and the choice of word that unerringly re-
creates the look, the feel, the smell of the thing, his gift for verbs
and adjectives that function physically, kinesthetically, to take
hold of us through our senses, through our bodies themselves. And
partly it is the effect of a quality less esthetic than moral—his
unflinching honesty, his refusal to evade or gloss over. His gift for
verbal re-creation of physical realities can be illustrated in poem
after poem. The following lines from "The Sentry" may serve as
an example:

> Rain, guttering down in waterfalls of slime,
> Kept slush waist-high and rising hour by hour,
> And choked the steps too thick with clay to climb.
> What murk of air remained stank old, and sour
> With fumes of whizz-bangs, and the smell of men
> Who'd lived there years, and left their curse in the den,
> If not their corpses . . .

The slimy wet, "guttering" down the mud walls of the trench and
soaking its inhabitants; the thick, sticky clay; the stink of fumes
and of bodies, living and dead are all vividly present to the senses.
The exhausted men of "Dulce et Decorum Est" are not figures in a
painting but real soldiers involved in a real war: "Bent double,

like old beggars under sacks,/Knock-kneed, coughing like hags, we cursed through sludge." And the gas casualty of the same poem is visibly and audibly suffering the throes of dissolution:

> . . . the white eyes writhing in his face,
> His hanging face, like a devil's sick of sin;
> If you could hear, at every jolt, the blood
> Come gargling from the froth-corrupted lungs . . .

In the pictures he paints of combat, his verbs and adjectives and adverbs are all active, concrete, often brutal: in "Greater Love" limbs are "knife-skewed"; in "Insensibility" the senses of soldiers have been "ironed" in "some scorching cautery of battle"; the fighting men of "Apologia Pro Poemate Meo" have "slashed bones bare"; the bayonets of "Arms and the Boy" are "famishing for flesh"; the frozen men, living and dead, of "Exposure" have their hands "shrivelled," their foreheads "puckered," and "all their eyes are ice." The eyeballs of the blinded man in "The Sentry" are "huge-bulged like squids'," and the troops in "The Show" are caterpillars in very truth: "I saw their bitten backs curve, loop, and straighten,/I watched those agonies curl, lift, and flatten."

His preference for the present participle is noticeable in nearly all his war poems, and it is largely this usage which imparts so much directness and immediacy to his scenes. The mad soldiers of "Mental Cases" are "Drooping tongues from jaws that slob their relish,/Baring teeth that leer like skulls' teeth wicked," for in their disordered minds, "Wading sloughs of flesh these helpless wander,/Treading blood from lungs that had loved laughter." The officer in the apocalyptic bombardment of "The Sentry" forgets the blinded casualty, "In posting Next for duty, and sending a scout/To beg a stretcher somewhere, and flound'ring about/To other posts under the shrieking air"; and the death of the soldier killed while asleep is described thus: "There was a quaking/Of the aborted life within him leaping. . . ."

Noticeable too is Owen's liking for inversion of the customary word order, his frequent placing of the adjective after rather than before its noun ("skulls' teeth wicked"), thus directing attention to and emphasizing the quality, the concrete physical presence of what he is describing. In his realistic poems he wrote with his eye fixed on the object, and between the thing or the event and the word there is no space, no room in which to evade reality.

Over and above this faithfulness to physical truth which dictated the choice of word and image, there is another sort of faithfulness: an unrelenting honesty of idea, of attitude, of emotion, which insists that the implications as well as the thing itself be fully realized. It was not merely his rejection of "poetry" which created the great war poems, but his rejection of his mother's comfortable and blind religious convictions and the insensitive and unreflecting optimism which they engendered. In "Asleep," for example, the dead soldier is presented as an object indistinguishable from the ground where he lies, no more than a part of physical nature and in his death one with all the past:

> —Or whether yet his thin and sodden head
> Confuses more and more with the low mould,
> His hair being one with the grey grass
> And finished fields of autumns that are old . . .

The slain soldier of "Strange Meeting" knows that the effect of war is irremediable:

> For of my glee might many men have laughed,
> And of my weeping something had been left,
> Which must die now.

The spiritual destruction of war's innocent victims must be fully and unflinchingly faced, sometimes gravely, as in "Insensibility"; sometimes with an almost Jacobean suggestion of the macabre, as in "Spring Offensive" and "The Send-Off." The men's physical destruction is never glorified or sentimentalized. It is portrayed with brutal accuracy when they "die as cattle," or are "blown to chops." And the degradation of cowardice or the death-in-life of madness is rendered in such images as "Lay stupid like a cod, heavy like meat," and the more imaginative and suggestive "thus their heads wear this hilarious, hideous,/Awful falseness of set-smiling corpses." Death himself is not the mysterious and august figure of Alan Seeger's "I Have a Rendezvous with Death" nor his effect Brooke's "white/Unbroken glory, a gathered radiance,/A width, a shining peace, under the night." He is a decomposing corpse offending the senses with "the green, thick odour of his breath."

VI *The Tommies Speak*

Twice Owen experimented with what amounts to dialect, the language of the British common soldier, producing effective poems which differ from the rest of his war poetry in language and viewpoint and differ from each other as well. "The Letter" and "The Chances" reveal even more strikingly than "Inspection" and "The Dead-Beat" his ear for the nuances of speech and his ability to handle conversational, colloquial verse. They reveal, too, his unsentimental but appreciative familiarity with the psychology of the men he led and fought beside. The perspective, like the language, in these poems is not that of poet or prophet, nor of officer educated and aware of the meaning of what is happening to him. The ordinary man, enduring his lot with what fortitude and resignation he can summon, speaks in these poems; and their emotion is not so much in him as in the reader.

"The Letter" is a deceptively simple poem, utterly realistic in tone, phrase, and in the homely details in which the soldier's thought of wife, family, and the past life of peacetime is counterpointed against the grim present of his precarious and short life in the trenches. It makes its effect by understatement and, as so many of Owen's poems do, by effective juxtaposition and contrast. The soldier's awkward reassurances, which are false and which he knows to be so, his rough solicitude and tenderness, his horseplay with comrades in the midst of battle and death, his forgetfulness of self—all make a picture of unassuming gallantry, of a chivalry that has nothing to do with class or convention, and evoke pity for the helplessness of this so-ordinary human being in the hell of war and admiration for his courage and his love.

"The Chances," equally true to life in vocabulary and manner, is more profound in its implications: its effect is closer to tragedy than to pathos. The very matter-of-factness with which the speaker recounts what happened, his down-to-earth point of view, make the last lines strike at the imagination with unforgettable force: " 'E's wounded, killed, and pris'ner, all the lot,/The bloody lot all rolled in one. Jim's mad." The soldier who speaks has no comment; he is apparently merely reminiscing, having been put in mind of a grimly ironic event he witnessed. But the reader supplies the comment, the pity, and terror for the fate of the youngster who, before battle, tried to bolster himself with homely stoicism. What, after all, could happen to him except death, wounds, or capture? One eventuality he overlooked, and like Nemesis, it has risen to destroy him. The poem is short, only eighteen lines; the voice, that of Everyman, his slang, his homespun philosophy, his wry courage; but behind its casual understatement we hear the accents of tragedy and experience something very like catharsis.

VII *Imagination and Vision*

The impact of Owen's vividly sensuous vocabulary and images makes it easy to overlook a fact which should not be forgotten: despite his gift for the concrete and the realistic, he is fundamentally an imaginative and a visionary poet. He is nowhere more characteristically himself than when he passes in word and image from the world of the senses to the world of the imagination, and at these times his gaze lifts from the mud and blood of battle and surveys the infinite reaches of the spirit. His use of balance and parallelism of phrase and clause, his effective contrasts, are not mere verbal tricks; they are the stamp of a mind which habitually viewed the visible, material world in the presence of the invisible but real world of spiritual values.

The weary men of "Insensibility" march—not with lame and bloody feet to their bivouac for the night, like those of "Dulce et Decorum Est"—to a more distant and a timeless resting place: "The long, forlorn, relentless trend/From larger day to huger night." In "Spring Offensive" the real scene melts into the symbolic as the more reflective soldiers stand still, "To face the stark, blank sky beyond the ridge,/Knowing their feet had come to the end of the world," and again when they enter battle, "the green slope/Chasmed and steepened sheer to infinite space," while those who died, "plunged and fell away past this world's verge." Sometimes the poet's imagination presents grotesque and macabre images, as when he personifies the weapons of war in "The Last Laugh" and "Arms and the Boy," analogizes the bodily attitudes of violent death in battle to those of sensual love in "Greater Love," sees mad soldiers as damned souls in hell, or the whole western front with its struggling troops as the decaying head of a corpse writhing with worms. Sometimes he produces an almost metaphysical conceit, like the pun in "Greater Love": "Heart, you were never hot/Nor large, nor full like hearts made great with shot"; a ghastly wit which at the same time shocks, describes with fidelity to physical fact, and makes vivid the poem's theme, the spiritual value of sacrifice.

Some of his most striking effects he obtains through suggestive incongruities and contrasts, juxtaposing two different worlds or presenting one reality in terms of another. "I, too, saw God through mud,—" he begins "Apologia Pro Poemate Meo," a poem which, like "Greater Love," contrasts the spiritual values of war with the more material ones of peace. In "Insensibility," "The front line withers/But they are troops that fade, not flowers," an image which is itself an ironic comment upon poetic images of death in battle. His greatest lines move the imagination and the soul, rather than shock the senses: "The pallor of girls' brows shall be their pall" says all there is to be said about grief, as "He's lost his colour very far from here" does about terror, and "Was it for this the clay grew tall?" is an unanswerable comment on war, at once question and judgment.

It is, perhaps, inevitable that Owen has not been, and he probably never will be, so well known and popular a poet as, say, Rupert Brooke; for craftsmanship is of more interest to the poet and the professional student of poetry than to the average reader. Owen's resolute refusal to glamorize or sentimentalize war prevents his poetry from appealing to cheap and easy notions of honor, glory, or patriotism; and his personal obscurity prevented him from appearing, like Brooke, as a symbol of gallant youth sacrificed on his country's altar. The slow growth of his reputation was not aided by overattention to his device of half-rhyme or overemphasis on his realism at the expense of his rarer achievements. Except by a handful of perceptive critics, writing for the most part in scholarly journals of small circulation, his poetry has been neglected and misunderstood. Even those who have read and appreciated it have tended to value it for reasons largely irrelevant or peripheral to its real value. Despite these handicaps, however, his poems have held their own, wearing ever and ever better by comparison with those of most of his contemporaries; and recently there have been signs that a truer understanding and appreciation of them is beginning. How they have fared in the fifty years since his death is the subject of the following chapter.

CHAPTER 5

Afterwards: The Growth of
Owen's Reputation

WHEN Rupert Brooke died at the age of twenty-seven in the early days of the war, it was widely felt, and said, that England had lost her most promising young poet. But on Wilfred Owen's death in 1918 no one could have predicted that fifty years later his fame as a poet would have begun to outshine Brooke's. The odds, indeed, against the mere survival of his poems were enormous. As has already been noted, most of his associates were unaware that he wrote poetry or had any aspirations toward poetic fame and achievement. Outside of his family, a mere handful of acquaintances, made for the most part in the last few months of his life, had read any of his verses; and even Siegfried Sassoon did not yet fully realize their quality. No evidence suggests that the four poems which had appeared in print had attracted any notice. The other verses existed only on odd bits of paper, many of them in different drafts or part-drafts with scribbled corrections and deletions so that the final version was often in doubt. Owen himself, of course, had not had time to revise or produce final copies of more than a few, or to take any additional steps toward his projected volume except to draft his short and enigmatic Preface and a table of contents indicating the topic headings under which he proposed to group separate poems.

A year later, in November, 1919, the sonnet "The End" was printed in *The Saturday Westminster Gazette,* and during the following months seven other poems, among them some of Owen's finest, appeared in various periodicals. Sassoon and Edith and Osbert Sitwell were responsible for these first steps toward introducing Owen's verse to the public, and also in winning posthumous recognition for his achievements. His first anthology appearance was in *Wheels: Fourth Cycle,* edited by Edith Sitwell, which, also in 1919, printed a group of seven poems: "Strange Meeting," "The Show," "A Terre," "The Sentry," "Disabled," "The

Dead-Beat," and "The Chances." That perspicacious literary critic John Middleton Murry at once detected the accents of a new, exciting, and important poet. Seizing particularly upon "Strange Meeting," he proclaimed it "the one fine poem in *Wheels*," and "the finest in these two books [the other was *Georgian Poetry, 1918–1919*], both in intention and achievement": "It touches great poetry by more than the fringe. Even in its technique there is the hand of the master to be. Those monosyllabic assonances are the discovery of genius. We are persuaded that this poem by a boy like his great forerunner [Keats], who had the certainty of death in his heart, is the most magnificent expression of the emotional significance of the war that has yet been achieved by English poetry. By including it in his book, the editor of *Wheels* has done a great service to English letters." [1]

Less than two years after his death, owing to the efforts of his mother and a few friends, Owen's genius had thus been recognized and publicly saluted. Shortly afterward, in December, 1920, the first edition of his poems, prepared from the manuscripts by Edith Sitwell and Siegfried Sassoon, was published. The reviews, some by fellow poets like Edmund Blunden and Robert Nichols, were for the most part very favorable and showed a discriminating appreciation of Owen's general qualities as a poet as well as of individual poems such as "Anthem for Doomed Youth," "Greater Love," "A Terre," and "Apologia Pro Poemate Meo." "Strange Meeting" seems always to have impressed all who read it with its extraordinary visionary power.

Following Murry's lead, reviews proclaimed Owen as the greatest poet of the war. "Owen steps at once from his obscurity to a place among the unchallengeable poets," [2] observed Sir John C. Squire; and Blunden, himself soldier and poet, testified that "He is first and foremost the witness of war's effect on the spirit of man," and called "Apologia" "the most satisfying and the truest proportioned analysis of the man in the trenches, and why he endured as he did, yet written." [3] An unsigned review in *The Spectator* compared Owen to Sassoon, whose reputation as a poet of the war stood high; and the reviewer announced that "had he [Owen] lived, one feels he had in him the makings of a finer poet than Mr. Sassoon will ever be, because his sense of compassion was so strong, and yet it never sank into sentimentality. . . . Mr. Owen might one day have written something great." [4] Guarded as this

statement now sounds, it was high praise in these early days for a
poet hitherto unknown.

Critics like Murry and poets like Blunden had at once perceived
the originality and effectiveness of Owen's diction and technical
devices, particularly half-rhyme, the most immediately obvious of
them. "The very make of his language is hard and remorseless or
strange and sombre as he wills; the discovery of final assonances
in place of rhyme may mark a new age in poetry," wrote Blunden.[5] An unsigned review of Sassoon's edition in *The London Mercury* exhibits a balanced appraisal of the new poet's techniques
and aims which might have been a lesson to some commentators
who came after him. "Every line betrays a passion for technical
experiment . . . but he knew all that was merely a discovery of
the best means to an end," the reviewer says; and then he pro-
ceeds to tell his readers what Owen meant by his Preface: "His
prime object was not fame or the satisfaction of creating beautiful
works of art, but the dedication of all his powers to the service of
one ideal, the propagation of the truth about war. . . . He wrote
out of an overwhelming love." [6]

The only faintly dissenting voice in this chorus of acclaim came
from the anonymous reviewer of *The Times Literary Supplement*
who, speaking perhaps for a broader average of readers, treated
both Owen's subject matter and his technique with cautious distaste. "A curious vagary of technique may be noted," he observed,
"in the writer's habit here and there . . . to use imperfect
rhymes," and he complained of the poet's lack of lyric grace and
poetic melody: "The writer is deeply oppressed by the repulsive
horrors of war as he has seen them; and he sets himself with grim
determination to get them into words . . . strong, stark statements wrenched, as it were, into rhyme and meter." [7]

Considering Owen's obscurity, the circumstances of his life and
death, and the state in which his verses had been left, he must be
considered fortunate indeed in the reception accorded his first
published poems. By and large, these early notices were perceptive and full of praise; and they introduced points which since
have been debated in more detail: the meaning of the Preface,
the nature and function of the poet's technical innovations, his
aims as a poet, his qualities of realism and of compassion.

I   *The 1920's*

The first impetus given to Owen's posthumous career, however, slackened as the 1920's wore on. Those who had suffered through the war preferred, naturally enough, to forget it until their memories had become less painful and their perspective clearer. Critics and reviewers were busy with other poets, other subjects, different techniques. Pound, Eliot, Yeats, the Imagists, Robinson, Frost, and a whole host of minor poets in England and America were writing, debating, and revolutionizing traditional attitudes, subject matter, forms, and methods. Young men, the poets of the next decade, were reading Owen and taking him to their hearts—not always for particularly relevant or valid reasons—but of critical attention there was little; and of interest among average readers of poetry (if there are any such) there was less.

In 1925 H. P. Collins included a chapter called "The War and Wilfred Owen" in his book *Modern Poetry,* pronouncing Owen and Hardy the only two poets whose "spiritual apprehension" spoke to a "critical generation that demands much," and judging "Strange Meeting" "the greatest very short poem written in our language in modern years." [8] Writing in *The Welsh Outlook* in 1928 Ifan Kyrle Fletcher claimed Owen as one of "our own Welshmen"—an error which has reappeared from time to time—declaring his achievement great and his promise "almost illimitable," and comparing him favorably to the more facile Rupert Brooke for emotional depth and clarity of expression.[9] And Henry Williamson, in a piece called "Reality in War Literature" printed in *The London Mercury* early in 1929, said that Owen was one "whom men of future ages will hail as the poet of the lost generation." [10] These voices were heard only faintly, however, amid the clamor of the day.

II   *The Beginning of Appreciation*

In 1931 a revised and enlarged edition of Owen's poems was published, edited by Edmund Blunden. Textually more accurate than Sassoon's edition, this collection included more than twice as many poems as the earlier volume; for the best of the juvenilia accompanied the war poems. Blunden's memoir of Owen's life and work, based largely on the poet's letters to his mother, still remains on the whole the fullest and best account yet published.

This volume took a long step forward in spreading knowledge of Owen's poetry, and it remained for more than thirty years the standard edition. Reprinted ten times in England, it was brought out in America in 1931 by the Viking Press, and it was reprinted in 1949 by New Directions. Since, according to Sassoon, the total number of copies printed of his edition was only 2,250, of which a mere 750 went to the United States,[11] it is obvious that Blunden's edition was much needed and that a great many readers must have encountered Owen for the first time in its pages.

Like the reviews of Sassoon's edition, those of Blunden's both in England and America were almost uniformly more than merely favorable; they were enthusiastic. Furthermore, considering the average quality of book reviews even in scholarly or literary periodicals, they show a surprising discernment. Almost unanimously the reviewers proclaim Owen the greatest poet of the war, pointing to his integrity, his "controlled anguish of mind," [12] his unsentimental pity, his "white hatred for the callous and unthinking," [13] his "economy and fierce concentration," [14] and the scale of his vision, by means of which he often attains "the effect called sublimity, the rarest virtue in English poetry." [15]

No longer were the critics nonplussed, like the earlier *The Times Literary Supplement* reviewer, by his technical innovations. "He found the perfect means of expression for his content," [16] said Alan Porter in *Voices;* and Stanley Kunitz, writing in *Poetry,* said that "No one before or since has employed assonance so habitually and understandingly, with such delight in the open vowel sounds and the inexhaustible supply of rich feminine endings." [17] An unsigned review in *The Spectator,* after describing Owen's use of assonance and half-rhyme, judged that he had "perfected [these devices] to a use of which one would hardly have suspected them adaptable; that is, to convey the frustration of the battlefields, the denials, the horror that became obscene in its intensity; and the quiet countermovement of the day-to-day spirit of endurance and comradeship, a tenderness greater than the love between man and wife." [18] A mild protest against too much attention to technique at the expense of more important aspects of Owen's poetry was entered by "Inconstant Reader" in *The Canadian Forum:* "much more has been said about the assonances in Wilfred Owen's poetry than about the passion and the mystery of it . . . the chance to use assonance again in Wilfred Owen's way and with his profound justification may not come again for years and years." [19]

The best of the reviews—those by Richard Church in the English *New Statesman and Nation* and by Theodore Morrison in the *Atlantic's* "Bookshelf"—emphasized the fact that Owen was not merely a war poet; his poetry was not limited in scope and meaning by immersion in a particular historical situation. Said Church: "Owen was a complete poet: that is to say, a man dedicating the whole of his powers, mental and spiritual, to poetry as a life-vocation, just as such masters as Milton, Wordsworth, Keats, and W. B. Yeats have done. His expression was not a mere outcry of youth over-stimulated by the cruel adventure and premature disillusionment of War." [20] Morrison struck the same note: "That he was one of the strongest, most deeply moving, most ironically and fiercely discerning spirits who spoke in abhorrence of war and in heart-rent pity for its victims can hardly be doubted. Yet from early youth, before the shadow fell, he was absorbed in learning the poet's art, and some day the small body of work which time allowed him to leave must be judged as poetry alone . . . an example of his more general poetic gifts is 'The End,' a sonnet which haunts the imagination with the echo of great tragedy in union with stern beauty." [21]

The only dissenting voice was Horace Gregory's. In a review entitled "A Dead Poetic Movement," in *The Nation*, he lumped Owen's verse with that of the Georgians in general; and he sourly consigned them all to oblivion, condemning the "patriotic rhetoric" of Brooke and the "hastily assumed realism" of Sassoon and Owen, declaring the latter's failure "characteristic of an entire movement in English poetry." [22] Gregory's criticism of the Georgians is sound enough, but he failed to realize how very un-Georgian Owen's poetry is.

During the 1930's, a number of thoughtful and perceptive essays established understanding and appreciation of Owen's poetry more firmly and on a higher level than had the reviews, which by their nature are—even the best of them—somewhat sketchy and superficial. The earliest of these was a long article by I. M. Parsons in *The Criterion*. Praising Owen for his "full-blooded squaring up to reality," his "terrifying" honesty, Parsons pointed out as well his understanding of the less tangible forces behind material phenomena: "He saw, as few saw clearly while the War was still in progress, the forces really at work—the whole gamut of self-deception which inevitably accompanies war on a large scale."

Parsons also drew attention to the complex nature and function of Owen's technical devices, the subtle cross-references, echoes, and anticipations, the integration of sound into the total meaning of the poem, and the poet's skill in handling rhythm. Having done full justice here, he adjudged Owen's true importance to lie not in his methods and innovations but in his purpose of propaganda—in the best sense, in the intellectual and emotional content of his verse which "is valuable because it expresses, in terms of poetry, a personal reaction to experiences which left most men inarticulate." [23] Parsons' was the fullest and best assessment of Owen's achievement that had yet appeared; and it still remains a valuable contribution to the rather small body of meaningful criticism of his work.

Writing in 1931, Parsons mentioned the fact that Owen's poetry was still relatively unfamiliar to a majority of readers, assigning as a reason for this, among others, that he "neither followed nor founded any school. . . . The influence of other poets in the later poems is traceable but difficult to specify, and certainly few have attempted to imitate his methods. Fortunately they do not lend themselves easily to imitation; they are the communication of an entirely individual experience and are themselves individual." [24] Two years later, however, *Authors Today and Yesterday*, edited by Stanley Kunitz, in summing up Owen's achievements as a poet, declared that "His experiments in prosody were held responsible for the increasing use of assonance as a variation to rhyme, among poets of the younger generation." [25] This seems to have been the first explicit recognition of the impact of Owen's poetry, and particularly of his auditory devices, upon the new generation of poets beginning to come into prominence.

III   *The "Pylon Poets" Discover Owen*

The precise nature and extent of Owen's influence on the poets of the 1930's and those who followed them has been much debated and variously estimated. "Influence" is always a difficult and delicate business to assess, and it is easier to indulge in critical truisms than to specify exactly in what it consists. That the 1930's poets copied Owen's technical devices, particularly half-rhyme, is obvious; that they adopted him as a kind of mascot, a symbol or avatar of certain ideas and attitudes of their own, is also plain; but that the deeper meaning of his own vision penetrated and affected the spirit of their poetry cannot be demonstrated.

What Owen meant to the writers who were growing up in the postwar England of the 1920's has been testified to by Stephen Spender, C. Day Lewis, Christopher Isherwood, and Louis Mac-Neice in their criticism and their autobiographies. In *A Hope for Poetry*, published in 1934, C. Day Lewis claimed Owen as one of the immediate ancestors of postwar poetry, along with Hopkins and Eliot; and he defined what seemed to these men his particular achievement and significance for those who followed: "Owen was a true revolutionary poet, opening up new fields of sensitiveness for his successors. If he had lived, there is no knowing what his promise might have achieved; he would have found, active in different guises, the cant, the oppression, the sufferings and courage which had challenged his powers during the war. As it is, his unsentimental pity, his savage and sacred indignation, are the best of our inheritance. . . ." [26]

In his autobiography *The Buried Day* published in 1960, Day Lewis describes his sense of immediate sympathy, almost of identification, with the poems of Owen when he first read them and what it was that he and friends like W. H. Auden and Spender felt they had in common with the earlier poet. "The new world some of us envisaged," says Day Lewis, "was one where the ties should be of flesh and blood, not of money and paper, and where the social system should have reintegrated the individual personality . . . we did not accept the values of our society . . . we were imagining through our poetry a society whose values the poet could identify himself with." [27] And in the introduction to his 1963 edition of Owen's *Collected Poems*, Day Lewis speaks again of Owen's great spiritual influence on the poets of his own generation. "It is Owen, I believe, whose poetry came home deepest to my own generation, so that we could never again think of war as anything but a vile, if necessary, evil." [28]

In a chapter entitled "Poetry and Pity" in his book *The Destructive Element* (1935), Spender paid tribute to Owen in terms which show even more clearly how this group of poets was claiming him as an elder brother, as a spokesman, had he lived, for the preoccupations and point of view characteristic of themselves. Owen's statement in his Preface, "All a poet can do today is warn," meant, Spender claims, that he realized his war poetry could only represent a transitional attitude, and that the next generation must occupy itself with different problems. Had Owen lived, he himself thus would have been concerned with the same problems that occupied the attention of Spender and his friends. "If Owen had survived the War, he would presumably have been compelled either to become a writer with some political philosophy, or else he must have harked back constantly to his war memories for inspiration. . . . Owen's poetry . . . exists by its reference to some external object: if it had not been the War, it might have been the industrial towns, and the distressed areas." [29]

In his autobiography, *World Within World* (1951), Spender speaks disparagingly of certain postwar writers, particularly the so-called Bloomsbury group, who considered politics alien to literature and who thought his own poetic generation barbarous because it "proclaimed that bourgeois civilization was at an end, and which assumed the certainty of revolution, which took sides and which was exposed even within its art to the flooding-in of outside public events. . . ." [30] Owen, of course, had been a poet whose art had been exposed to "the flooding-in of outside public events" and equally of course would have been the poet of revolutionary social and political issues had he survived.

Christopher Isherwood who, like Spender, had been introduced to Owen's poetry by W. H. Auden, strikes a note of even more appealing naïveté in his autobiography *Lions and Shadows* (1947). During the time of the General Strike in England, in 1926, he says: "I hated myself, too, for being neutral . . . I found myself opening Wilfred. He, at least, had understood what I was feeling: 'Waving good-bye, doubtless they'd told the lad . . .' But Wilfred hadn't buried his disgust in the cushions of a Kensington drawing room; or tried vainly to pretend that as an intellectual he belonged to some mystical Third Estate, isolated above the battle." [31]

These young men, Auden, Day Lewis, Spender, MacNeice, and Isherwood were still schoolboys when they first encountered Owen's verse in the 1920's; and in the 1930's, when they were beginning to dominate English poetry, they had already adopted the elder poet as an earlier comrade in art and in the struggle for social justice—for a world in which the institutions of society should serve personal and individual ends. Owen had seen through the pretensions of authority to the hypocrisy and cruelty beneath. He had stood for human values, sacrificed to the inhuman and mechanical power of the State. He had deliberately dedicated his art to the service of truth instead of remaining detached and aloof. He had himself participated in the action and suffering of his times, and he had been martyred by "the gang" in power. Their practice of referring to him by his Christian name shows how closely they felt him to be identified with them in spirit and in purpose.

Whether they were justified in feeling such an identification is very doubtful; but it is not particularly relevant to a consideration of Owen's actual influence on them. That Owen would ever have been a Marxist, like Spender and Day Lewis in the 1930's, is difficult to believe. Despite his capacity for anger at cruelty, waste, and hypocrisy, he disliked orthodoxy and institutional attitudes whether in politics or religion; and there was nothing either fanatical or doctrinaire about his mind. He would have found it easier to believe in original sin than in the class struggle, and to embrace the Church rather than the Party. His was an imaginative and visionary mind which tended to see particular events in terms of universal meanings and values; and, had he turned to social and political issues he would surely have treated them as, in his best poems, he did his experiences of war: as the symbol and microcosm of a more general human dilemma, the dilemma of man suffering amid the contradictions of his own nature and the perplexities of an alien and indifferent universe.

Of the poets of this group, it is Spender who most exhibits the influence of Owen's spirit, not merely his methods. James G. Southworth noted this in an essay written not long after *The Destructive Element:*

Much of the love which Mr. Spender had for his fellows is the direct outgrowth of pity. It is here that the political aspect of his poetry is most evident . . . he experiences more acutely than does the average man the hopeless welter of present-day chaos.

Pity is the keynote of Wilfred Owen's poetry and of his influence on Mr. Spender. He has revealed to a brother artist its possible use in poetry. In Owen's case it was the pity of war; in Mr. Spender's, the pity toward the victims of the post-war conditions.[32]

This is true; yet let us compare, for example, Owen's "Futility" with Spender's "Ultima Ratio Regum"—certainly one of the latter poet's finest pieces, coming out of his experiences in Spain during the Civil War. The theme of both poems is the same: the death of a young soldier in battle. The emotions of Spender's poem are Owen's own characteristic blend of anger and compassion. His tone, like Owen's, is calm and controlled, almost dispassionate, until it rises at the end, again like Owen's, to passionate and lyrical protest. He employs the same rhetorical devices in his last stanza as does the second stanza of "Futility":

> Consider his life which was valueless
> In terms of employment, hotel ledgers, news files.
> Consider. One bullet in ten thousand kills a man.
> Ask. Was so much expenditure justified . . .

But, where Owen sees the young man's death as a mockery of all creation—a negation of the age-old processes which have toiled to bring him into being—Spender appeals to a capitalist economy which operates in terms of the profit motive and which has, in killing the young soldier, invested its money unwisely since his life had no value to the system. Both poets champion the human values of youth, life, and love against the forces which destroy them; but the war which kills Owen's soldier is not seen by the poet as the outcome of a specific economic and social system, as Spender sees it. Owen places his soldier in a universal, Spender his in a particular context. It is a question of perspective and emphasis, of the tone and make of a man's mind. "Spiritual" is a much abused word, but it is the only word that fits Owen's outlook, and this quality sets him apart from the poets of the 1930's as it does from his fellow war poets. We have only to consider Owen's poem "Miners" and ask what the Pylon Poets would have done with such a subject if we wish to recognize that, whatever the nature of Owen's influence, it did not touch the spirit of their verse. His is a poetry both more simple and more profound than theirs, and the truths he had to tell were not of particular systems but of the human condition.

Spender does, however, indicate in his autobiography an effect which Owen's poetry, along with many other influences, must have helped to accelerate in modern verse: "I began to realize that unpoetic-seeming things were material for poetry . . . what excited me about the modern movement was the inclusion within new forms of material which seemed ugly, anti-poetic, and inhuman . . . these [he is speaking especially of Joyce's *Ulysses* and Eliot's *The Waste Land*] showed me that modern life could be material for art, and that the poet, instead of having to set himself apart from his time, could create out of an acceptance of it." [33] That Owen had wrought poetry out of obscene ugliness and horror was his particular triumph, and it must have been a lesson not lost on these men who set themselves to depict and master poetically the almost equal ugliness and horror of the postwar wasteland.

If Owen's vision failed to inform the poetry of the 1930's, the influence of his experiments with assonance and half-rhyme is clear and unquestionable. Auden, Spender, Day Lewis, and MacNeice all were led by his example to experiment themselves with these devices; and their early verse in particular furnishes numerous examples of them. But for the very reason that Owen's technical influence upon them is readily detectable and has been reiterated by commentators on their poetry, a caveat must be entered.

None of these poets used Owen's methods with the consistency and subtlety that he displayed, and none of them achieved through the use of these devices the effects that he achieved. John Bayley is right in saying that assonance with Owen was not so much technical as it was part of the movement of his mind,[34] and Louis MacNeice is right when he says that Owen used his technical innovations "consciously or unconsciously for a certain purpose and they fitted it like a glove." [35] As we have already seen, Owen's sound effects at their most successful directly reinforce the content, tone, and general impact of the poem and cannot be disentangled from the whole. But Auden's use of alliteration, half-rhyme, and consonance, in such early poems as "The Journey" and "The Three Companions" seems more facile than integral to the poem's meaning and effect; and even Day Lewis, though he regularly uses half-rhyme with great skill and subtlety, never produces such symphonic effects as Owen did in "Insensibility," for example. And, as these poets moved into maturity and found their own voices, they tended to use such devices less and less. Monroe K. Spears in his recent book *The Poetry of W. H. Auden* mentions Owen among others as an influence, but he tells us that "Once

Auden's own style, or styles, had been formed, however, the influences fade into the background; even as early as the 1928 *Poems* there is nothing derivative or imitative in the manner of the juvenile work." [36]

On the whole, then, it is difficult to see that Owen's poetry was as great an influence on that of the 1930's as is commonly claimed. David Daiches, one of Owen's most sympathetic and perceptive critics, in an essay written in 1936, pointed out in somewhat severe terms that the content of Owen's poetry had not influenced these poets at all; only his use of half-rhyme: "Owen is claimed by some modern poets as an important influence on their poetry, but it is difficult to see how Owen's poetry can influence those who have so much less to say." [37] But, if their fellow-feeling for him had not much basis in actual fact, and if the spirit of his verse did not noticeably impinge upon and alter the tone of their own, their adoption of him as a sort of mascot infuriated a poet greater than any of them and produced results which did affect (though not in the long run for the worse) Owen's poetic fortunes and reputation.

IV *Yeats and* The Oxford Book of Modern Verse

W. B. Yeats wrote in his Preface to the *Oxford Book of Modern Verse* (1936) which he edited:

I have a distaste for certain poems written in the midst of the great war; they are in all anthologies, but I have substituted Herbert Read's *End of a War* written long after. The writers of these poems were invariably officers of exceptional courage and capacity, one a man constantly selected for dangerous work, all, I think, had the Military Cross; their letters are vivid and humorous, they were not without joy . . . but felt bound, in the words of the best known, to plead the suffering of their men. In poems that had for a time considerable fame, written in the first person, they made that suffering their own. I have rejected these poems for the same reason that made Arnold withdraw his *Empedocles on Etna* from circulation; passive suffering is not a theme for poetry. . . . When man has withdrawn into the quicksilver at the back of the mirror no great event becomes luminous in his mind; it is no longer possible to write *The Persians, Agincourt, Chevy Chase:* some blunderer has driven his car on to the wrong side of the road—that is all.

If war is necessary, or necessary in our time and place, it is best to forget its suffering as we do the discomfort of fever. . . .[38]

The omission of Owen from this volume occasioned widespread criticism, and Yeats was taken severely to task by most of its reviewers. Astonished at the furor raised by Owen's admirers, he made no public rejoinder but defended himself privately and petulantly in a letter, since notorious, written to Dorothy Wellesley: "When I excluded Wilfred Owen, whom I consider unworthy of the poets' corner of a country newspaper, I did not know I was excluding a revered sandwich-board man of the revolution. . . . He is all blood, dirt, and sucked sugar-stick. . . ."[39] These two passages furnish the clues to Yeats's objection to Owen, but some knowledge of the great Irish poet's work and of his theories about art and its relation to life helps to clarify his feelings.

Throughout all Yeats's changes in style, method, and personality he exhibited, as his biographer and critic Richard Ellmann tells us, a consistency and tenacity in his fundamental attitudes and beliefs. And his one most basic and persistent belief was that the human mind had power to control the universe, to make and unmake reality. As a boy, he dreamed of controlling the world by a magician's wand; as an old man, he cried out, "I make the truth." In his youth, he wanted an art dedicated to the service of heroic dreams, and in his early verse he created and glorified a dream world, inventing an elaborate machinery of symbols whose professed object was to evoke an unseen reality, but whose real function was to hide this world rather than to reveal another. Myth and metaphor enabled him to bypass the question of literal belief; and, though he himself became involved in a life of action, his poetry remained essentially uninvolved in the questions that were agitating Ireland and the world around him. "To him," says Ellmann, "this life of action is tolerable only because it seems to him a supreme artifice";[40] and Yeats himself, in an essay on the *Noh* drama, declares: "All imaginative art keeps at a distance, and that distance once chosen must be held against a pushing world."[41]

In his later poetry, he spoke less and less often in his own person; instead, he used a variety of personae—beggars, hermits, and fools—"to voice with safety opinions about life and afterlife that he is not prepared to guarantee."[42] And, though he said that he had given up his old coat, embroidered with mythologies, and was "walking naked," his search was increasingly for "a variety of dramatic situations in which to pretend to be naked."[43] Believing that, though the man himself was always involved, his art should not be involved—that art was indeed an antidote to rather than an expression of his own involvement—he used his personae as a means of controlling a too-personal voice, of refining and objecti-fying his "accidence." In his "A General Introduction for My Work," written in 1937, Yeats stated his concept of an effective personae:

A poet writes always of his personal life, in his finest work out of its tragedy, whatever it be, remorse, lost love, or mere loneliness; he never speaks directly as to someone at the breakfast table, there is always a phantasmagoria. . . . Even when the poet seems most him-self . . . he is never the bundle of accident and incoherence that sits down to breakfast; he has been reborn as an idea, something in-tended, complete. A novelist might describe his accidence, his inco-herence, he must not; he is more type than man, more passion than type. . . . He is part of his own phantasmagoria and we adore him because nature has grown intelligible, and by so doing a part of our creative power.[44]

Yeat's great poems "The Tower," "Among School Children," and "Sailing to Byzantium" are what Ellmann calls "a defiant, Faustian cry of the infinite power of the mind of man." [45] "Among School Children" declares that only images made by the imagi-nation escape the disintegration of time, they only are real; and his all-encompassing belief in soul, self, or imagination (terms he used interchangeably) brought him to assert in his later poems the virtual identity of the universe created by the imagination with reality itself.

It is no wonder, then, that Yeats said: "We should not attribute a very high degree of reality to the Great War." [46] And it is no won-der that he had "a distaste" for Owen and his fellow war poets. Poetry for Yeats could not reside in some large general event, like war, or in an emotion, like pity, outside the author's control. He is the supreme exemplar in our time not so much of "art for art's sake" as of the world for art's sake. "Words alone are certain good," he had said as early as 1889;[47] and he came finally to be-lieve that words alone were real.

"Passive suffering" as a theme for poetry he despised because it was incompatible with his vision of the almighty power of man's mind, implying as it did a submission to a reality outside man's creation and command. Owen's declaration in his Preface that "The Poetry is in the pity" and his purpose of propaganda, of telling the truth about war, must have been anathema to Yeats. Poetry did not *tell* the truth so much as *create* the truth through imaginative power. The pity, Yeats would have said, is in the poetry. But esthete that he was, caring only for art and glorifying passion and power, he lacked compassion as much as he lacked humility. His attitude toward life and toward art was thus diametrically opposed to that of Owen, who explicitly repudiated estheticism, thought pity the only redemptive feature of war, and revealed in his poetry an extraordinary capacity for identification with the sufferings of others.

Yeats's "Second Coming" and Owen's "Strange Meeting" furnish an instructive comparison of the attitudes and of the theories of the two poets.[48] Both are prophetic poems, chronologically close and startlingly similar in their vision of the future, the fate of man in history. Though it cannot be precisely dated, "Strange Meeting" belongs to the last few months of Owen's life; "The Second Coming" was published in *Michael Robartes and the Dancer* in 1921. Both prophesy chaos to come, war, blood, and bestiality —the devastation of all human and Christian values. But in their tone and in their attitude toward the vision they present the poems differ.

Yeats's poem, though charged with excitement, is impersonal and objective. He is a seer and a recorder, predicting the end of the Christian era and the domination not of the God-Man but of the God-Beast. His condemnation of anarchy and bestiality is implicit in the terms he uses, but he remains uninvolved, a spectator, not a participant, envisioning "the blood-dimmed tide" but revealing no compassion for those overwhelmed by it. Owen, on the other hand, is involved as intimately as possible in the action and feeling of "Strange Meeting." His is the guilt, and his is the pity for the suffering of men and for the spiritual impoverishment of the world. And he sees the poet explicitly as prophet, almost as Savior, who would have washed away blood and violence "Even with truths that lie too deep for taint." Each poet predicts and defines the human historical situation; but, where Yeats merely records, Owen participates in, condemns, and renounces the brutalization they both foresee.

Yeats's letter to Dorothy Wellesley would seem to indicate that he had not realized to what an extent the poets of the 1930's had identified Owen with their own viewpoint and purposes until informed by the reviews of his anthology. When he did realize that, in his own words, Owen had become "a revered sandwich-board man of the revolution," it could only have strengthened his distaste for the latter's poetry and his determination to exclude it from his collection of modern verse. His political views differed from those of the Pylon Poets; and their notions of the social function of poetry, like Owen's purpose of propaganda, he detested. Their adoption of Owen could only have confirmed his own natural and instinctive antipathy to theories and attitudes so different from his own.

Yeats's jeer about the "sucked sugar-stick" quality of Owen's verse implies another and very likely quite unconscious reason for his hostility. It is a truism of psychology that people tend to dislike others for qualities they recognize and condemn in themselves. In Owen's early verse, and occasionally even in his late poems, Yeats could not have avoided recognizing something of his own youthful diction. Owen, who knew and admired Yeats's early poetry, had selected passages from Yeats to serve as epigraphs for his own poems "The Show" and "S.I.W." Owen's juvenile verses, like Yeats's earlier work, are full of dreams; of soft, sweet rhythms; and of lush, highly ornamental diction. These qualities Yeats was pruning from his poems to attain the spare, hard, stripped vocabulary and taut rhythms of his later verse. Owen too had emerged from dreams and was speaking as a man to men; but Yeats must have detected in Owen's work something of those qualities he was expunging from his own. This factor would account for the edge of emotion, the very personal dislike for Owen's poetry which he could not conceal. Doubtless it lent an extra dimension to his theoretical opposition to Owen's concept of the nature and function of poetry.

It is not, then, so surprising as at first sight it seems that Yeats did not and could not recognize the quality of Owen's poetry. To him, it would have seemed too subjective and personal on the one hand and, on the other, too submissive to and immersed in material circumstances to which "we should not attribute a very high degree of reality." It was informed by a spirit of pity foreign to his own nature, and had as its avowed purpose the telling of the objective truth about an objective event—war. It was written by a man who was being hailed as spiritual brother by a group of left-wing poets dedicated to using their art for social ends. And it betrayed here and there the same youthful luxuriance and languor that Yeats had repudiated in his own verse. Great poet that he was, and perhaps for that very reason, Yeats was a most indifferent judge of poetry. Always he sought not the principle of its own being but the presence or confirmation of the ideas and attitudes through which he was enabled to make his own great poems. *The Oxford Book of Modern Verse* is a monument to the idiosyncratic nature of his judgment.

V *Recognition and Acceptance*

In the long run, Yeats's exclusion of Owen from his anthology has done more damage to his own reputation as a critic than it has to Owen's as a poet. In fact, by directing attention to Owen's poetry and rousing indignation on his behalf, Yeats probably aided the growth of his reputation. Certainly since *The Oxford Book of Modern Verse* no anthology that includes early twentieth-century poetry has been considered complete without him. Owen's growing importance is testified to by the place his poems hold in recent collections like *Up the Line to Death* (1964) and *Men Who March Away* (1965), in which thirteen of his war poems are printed. Both of these anthologies include long notes on his achievements as a poet.

Nor is critical attention confined to the makers of anthologies or to articles appearing in somewhat obscure scholarly journals. Such influential critics as Edwin Muir, David Daiches, William York Tindall, Carl and Mark Van Doren, H. V. Routh, F. W. Bateson, Ifor Evans, Vivian de Sola Pinto, Hoxie Neale Fairchild, and Bonamy Dobrée have paid Owen tribute in terms that show a remarkable unanimity of opinion.[49] Their verdict is that Wilfred Owen is the greatest of the poets who wrote during and of World War I and that he is also one of the great poets of this century. Particularly have fellow poets fallen under his spell; Dylan Thomas, Lawrence Durrell, Edith and Osbert Sitwell, Allen Tate and Edmund Blunden, as well as Spender, Day Lewis, and MacNeice, have written appreciations of his work.[50]

In 1956 a fresh and striking proof was offered of the particular power with which Owen's poetry has appealed to fellow artists in the publication by the Gehenna Press of thirteen of Owen's poems with drawings by Ben Shahn. This beautiful edition, of which only four hundred copies have been printed, contains fifteen drawings illustrating a rather arbitrary selection of poems, including one fragment, "As bronze may be much beautified . . ." and also several of the poems in Owen's early manner, as well as "Miners" and such great war poems as "Futility," "Spring Offensive," "Greater Love," and "Strange Meeting." The principle appears to be simply the appeal of the poem to the artist's graphic imagination, and the volume is altogether more remarkable for the beauty of its type and the power of its drawings than for more literary reasons. A portrait of Owen, wood engraved from the drawing by Shahn and printed from the wood block, is the frontispiece and is one of the most arresting of the drawings. This expensive and limited edition could have done little to further popular knowledge of Owen's verse, but it is an attractive work of art in itself; and, like *War Requiem* a few years after, it furnishes evidence that Owen's is poetry for the poet, the artist, and the musician.

In the last few years a series of events have joined to bring Owen's name into greater prominence than before. The first of these was the publication in 1960 of D. S. R. Welland's book *Wilfred Owen: A Critical Study,* published in England by Chatto and Windus and reprinted in Canada by Clarke, Irwin and Company, Ltd. This study, the outgrowth of Dr. Welland's doctoral dissertation in the University of Nottingham, was the first and up to this time remains the only monograph on Owen that has appeared. Although, as one reviewer complained, the book "suffers from a lack of sharp, focusing and consecutive development," [51] it contained important scholarly and to a lesser extent critical material. For the first time, Owen's early verse was discussed in some detail, the probable source of half-rhyme in the poetry of Jules Romains suggested, and the problems connected with the text and dating of poems indicated. The book's most notable weakness from a scholarly point of view was its wholly inadequate bibliography.

In 1962 Benjamin Britten, the English composer and conductor, set some of Owen's most memorable war poems to music and combined them with the traditional Latin Mass for the Dead to make *War Requiem,* first performed in Coventry Cathedral on May 30, 1962. The work has since been performed in Westminster

Abbey and the Albert Hall in London, in West Berlin, and at Tanglewood, Massachusetts; each time it has been given an enthusiastic welcome. It has been televised, and it is now available in an excellent recording by the London Symphony Orchestra, conducted by Britten himself. William Plomer, who has writtten a short but very perceptive analysis and appreciation of Owen's poetry as Preface to the text of the *War Requiem*, declares Owen "the outstanding English poet of the First World War, and, because the Second World War was a continuation of it, of that too." *War Requiem* has done much to make Owen known to many who do not usually read either poetry or criticism.

The following year, 1963, saw the publication of a new edition of Owen's poems, edited by an old admirer, C. Day Lewis. Though not a full critical text, this volume prints many more of the juvenilia than did Blunden's edition, with notes on some of the variants and changes in successive drafts of poems, makes a number of emendations of Blunden's text, and includes Blunden's 1931 Memoir as well as Day Lewis's own Introduction. It was published in London, in New York, and in Toronto; and it has since been reprinted several times in each country.

In the same year appeared the first volume of Harold Owen's three-volume autobiography, *Journey from Obscurity*, subtitled *Wilfred Owen 1893–1918*. The first volume, *Childhood*, deals with the fortunes of the Owen family up to the summer of 1911; the second, *Youth*, which appeared in the following year, brings them to the beginning of the war in 1914; and the third, *War*, published in 1965, to a year or so after the end of World War I. The three volumes represent an astonishing performance of memory, insight, warmth, and sensitive sympathy and make a major contribution to the social history of a period. The subtitle *Wilfred Owen 1893– 1918* is not altogether accurate, for these books are about the Owen family and their life in the England of the early twentieth century. Harold himself, his parents, his other brother and sister, their family and friends, their schools and family activities, their economic struggle and efforts to make a start in life against heavy odds—all these are as important as Wilfred himself, and make an absorbing chronicle of a cultivated English provincial family fallen upon hard times. Harold's relationship with his elder brother, one of genuine love but acute sibling rivalry, is drawn with scrupulous detail, objectivity, and unquenchable affection; and Wilfred lives

in his pages "in his habit, as he was." It is a fascinating portrait of
a gifted, ambitious, and very far from perfect young man that
emerges. Any reader of Owen's war verse will find himself wondering afresh at the alchemy that transformed this self-absorbed,
rather precious, and spoiled favorite son, wrapped up in himself
and his dreams and ambitions, into the author of "Futility," and
"Anthem. . . ."

Day Lewis' edition and Harold Owen's memoirs of 1963 were
followed in 1964 and 1965 by the two anthologies of World War I
poems already mentioned, *Up the Line to Death* and *Men Who
March Away,* and there was published also in 1964 an important
critical study, *English Poetry of the First World War,* by John H.
Johnston, in which Owen's work likewise played a prominent
part. In 1965 appeared Patric Dickinson's autobiography, *The
Good Minute,* which discusses in detail Owen's influence on Dickinson's own life and poetry; Robert H. Ross's *The Georgian Revolt
1910–1922,* a study of the verse of that period; Frederick Grubb's
A Vision of Reality; and Bernard Bergonzi's *Heroes' Twilight: A
Study of the Literature of the Great War. Wilfred Owen. Collected Letters,* edited by Harold Owen and John Bell, was published in 1967 by the Oxford University Press, and constitutes the
most important recent contribution to a fuller knowledge of the
poet's life and personality.

The Victorian and Edwardian periods in literature are only now
beginning to be evaluated in a longer and more just perspective;
and it therefore seems reasonable to assume that there will be
many reassessments of literature in the immediate future and
many attempts on the part of a generation born during or just
after World War I to explore and understand the many aspects of
the conflict that ended—as mere chronology had not—the long
day's journey of the nineteenth century. At this time, Owen's reputation as a first-rate if relatively minor poet appears secure. A
final estimate of his achievement—if anything approaching final-
ity can be reached, since each age must re-evaluate works of art
for itself—depends on the answer we give to questions often
raised but difficult to settle; and to these we must now turn.

CHAPTER 6

Achievement

S URVIVAL is the final and most stringent test of poetry or of any art. That Wilfred Owen's verse survived the precarious circumstances of its gestation and birth is in itself a wonder. That it won immediate and enthusiastic recognition is more than might have been expected. That knowledge and appreciation of it have spread slowly but steadily through the years, and that the poet's reputation today stands higher than ever, are also persuasive witnesses to the enduring power of his vision, his spirit, and his skill. Poetry that shines with increasing luster for half a century has demonstrated more than an ephemeral value.

Owen's achievement and stature as a poet, however, have not yet been settled beyond question. Issues that were raised by early reviewers and critics and that were being debated twenty and thirty years ago are still alive. Were Owen's attitudes and techniques adequate to depict and evaluate modern warfare with all its implications? Or was his poetry too limited in form and too restricted by a narrowly personal and subjective point of view to achieve the artistic possibilities inherent in his subject? Did his pacifism limit the scope and meaning of his work? Are his poems weakened or invalidated by inadequacies of personality and temperament? Or, on the other hand, was his verse too detached from the personal and from the ordinary experiences of ordinary men? By insisting in his Preface on the poet's duty to warn, on the function of poetry as propaganda, was Owen demanding, as a recent critic has charged, "an over-simplification of the poet's task"? [1] How does his work compare with that of his contemporaries and fellow war poets? In the perspective of these fifty years, what is our verdict on his rank as a poet?

I *War Then and Now*

It takes a generation or longer for the work of any period to appear in reasonably clear perspective, and adequate appraisal of the World War I poets has only recently begun. The fullest and most thoughtful re-evaluation that has yet appeared is Professor John H. Johnston's *English Poetry of the First World War* (1964). In an introductory chapter, "Foreground and Background," Johnston considers "The Early Poets," Rupert Brooke, Julian Grenfell, Robert Nichols, and Charles Sorley, as a group; and he then devotes a chapter apiece to Sassoon, Blunden, Owen, Isaac Rosenberg, Herbert Read, and David Jones. "The standards invoked," says Johnston, "are those of the epic and heroic literature—the traditional literature of war." [2] By these standards, both of form and of content and attitude, he finds most of these poets, including Owen, deficient in their response to the possibilities of their subject and hence in what they were able to achieve poetically. "Most of the war poets," he says, "through their almost exclusive reliance on the contemporary lyric response and on the attitudes and techniques inherent in that response, were seriously hampered in their efforts to depict and evaluate their experiences, . . . [The] modern war lyric . . . was probably the medium least capable of dealing with the vastly multiplied moral and physical confusions of technological warfare." [3]

Read and Jones alone are exempted from this verdict. Read's long poem "The End of a War" and Jones's poetic narrative "In Parenthesis," Johnston considers successful examples of the "most significant feature of postwar verse . . . the change from the brief lyric mode to the long philosophic poem and to the heroic narrative. . . . [The] emphasis falls on the more universal aspects of violence and evil . . . [and] the formal artistic intention is that of relating the experience of modern warfare to the values implicit in the general range of human experience." [4] Jones's long poem is, Johnston says, "the only poetry of the war that is not distorted by ephemeral emotions or limited by subjective attitudes." [5]

Johnston admits that Owen "seemed to realize the limitations of a narrowly subjective or experiential approach. . . . By controlling the subjective element in his verse, Owen sought a greater freedom, exploring the larger moral and spiritual aspects of the conflict." [6] However, that Owen succeeded in producing great poetry he does not concede: "Despite Owen's extraordinary sensitivity and his efforts to reconcile that sensitivity to the demands of formal poetic art, his achievement does not measure up to the vast tragic potentialities of his material. . . . Unless pity is generated and objectified within a large tragic context, it cannot of itself support a tragic vision." [7]

It will be seen that these comments have much in common with Yeats's verdict on the same poets in his Introduction to *The Oxford Book of Modern Verse:* "When man has withdrawn into the quicksilver at the back of the mirror no great event becomes luminous in his mind." [8] In that anthology Yeats chooses, like Johnston after him, Read's "The End of a War," together with Julian Grenfell's "Into Battle," to represent the poetry of World War I. Yeats emphasizes what he considers the unduly personal and subjective element in the verse he rejects, whereas Johnston gives equal weight to what he judges the inadequacies of the lyric mode, but the basic position of the two men is the same.

First of all, it must be said that neither Yeats nor Johnston really objects to the presence of personal emotion as such in war poetry. What they dislike is the particular emotions the poets of the First World War felt and expressed. To Yeats only the joy of battle was a fit emotion for expression in poetry. But the joy of battle is as personal and subjective an emotion as pity, or rather more so. Johnston deplores the absence of the old-fashioned heroic spirit. The same comment applies. The difficulty is not the mere presence of personal emotion; it is the fact that Yeats and Johnston consider some emotions appropriate to war poetry and others not.

But men who had experienced modern technological warfare knew that the heroic spirit and the joy of battle were not merely inappropriate; they were wholly false to the realities of the trenches. Their emotions were different from those of earlier warriors like the thanes of the "Battle of Maldon" because warfare and its implications were different. Joy of battle is possible when men are matched against men, not when they are mangled by machines. Patriotism and the heroic spirit are possible when men are defending their land against barbarian invasion, not when they suspect politicians of making and prolonging war for sordid ends.

The poets of the trenches could not write in the old epic manner, nor with the joy of Grenfell, nor with the detachment of Read and Jones. Grenfell was killed early in the war and only briefly experienced its realities. Read and Jones both wrote long after the event. By then Read could explore large philosophical issues of man's nature and his relation to ultimate reality in a poem remarkable for its contemplative and somewhat abstract power, and Jones could link the experiences of an infantry battalion with those of other men in other wars and thus attempt to present World War I in the long and epic context of human history. Both poems are in their different ways interesting and successful—though "In Parenthesis" is poetic fiction rather than poetry—but they could not have been written years earlier in the trenches. If anguish and pity for suffering and revulsion against bestiality and waste are not fit subjects for poetry, poets at that time had no choice but to be silent. Yeats and Johnston appear to think they would have done better to be silent, rather than try to express what for them was the truth of modern warfare.

But the real question is not whether such emotions as pity and anguish are inappropriate to war poetry. No emotion in itself is inappropriate, no experience too personal and private for expression in poetry. The question is to what extent the poet has succeeded in freeing his emotion and his experience from the private and isolated world of himself, in giving it significant form, and so relating it to and revealing through it common and universal truths of human experience.

Despite the judgments of Yeats and Johnston, it is just this universalizing quality of Owen's genius which, in his greatest poems, is most apparent. As David Daiches says, "He wrote poetry for the sake of life, in order to reach out through the facts of war to fundamental aspects of human thought and emotion." [9] Owen's experience of war was the material through which he revealed his vision of man's nature, his relationship to his fellows, and to the universe itself. He was repelled by the insensibility of which the human heart is capable; this insensibility was revealed to him in the particular conditions of a particular war. He pitied all suffering, all waste, all guilt; he saw particular instances of suffering, waste, and guilt in the atrocities soldiers committed and suffered. His vision was greater than he himself knew, greater than his announced purpose of striking a blow at the conscience of England.

and the world. In such poems as "Strange Meeting," "The Show," "Insensibility," and "Futility," he freed himself wholly from the limitations of the personal and the subjective and gave form and body to universal truths. His pity *was* "generated and objectified within a large tragic context" and could therefore "support a tragic vision." His truths may be different from the truths of the traditional poetry of war, but who can maintain that they are less true and less valid than the martial valor of "Agincourt"?

These poems of Owen's just named are in themselves a sufficient answer to the critics who charge that his pacifism weakens his achievement as a poet. A reviewer of Day Lewis's edition of Owen's poems says, "We do not honour him the less for this [his pacifism], but it strengthens the historical limitations that attend his work." [10] But whether we agree with Owen or not that war is always and utterly evil is irrelevant to a judgment of his poetry. We cannot quarrel with his vision of what war does to the spirit of man, whether it is politically justifiable or not. We may argue that the consequences of war must be accepted lest worse ensue; we cannot deny that the consequences are always evil. Unless, indeed, we argue that the poet's vision of man as lover and creator is false, that he is brother to the wolf and the tiger rather than to Christ and that it is good for him to behave like a beast though he must suffer like a man, we cannot justly say that Owen's pacifism is an "historical limitation" on his verse. His pacifism was the result of his vision. And his vision at its clearest was not limited to the trenches of World War I but saw man and the world *sub specie aeternitatis.*

The charge of Yeats and Johnston that Owen's poetry is obsessed wth "passive suffering," and that the "passivity" of his attitude limits him as a poet has recently been reiterated in a review of Day Lewis's edition appearing in *The Times Literary Supplement.* This reviewer complains also of Owen's "almost God-like" detachment and distance from the personal and the ordinary.[11] At first sight these criticisms seem directly opposed to the more usual charge of overrealism and immersion in the particular and the personal, the falsity of which we have seen; but they rest on an equal failure to apprehend the nature of Owen's war poems.

About Owen's "passivity" there are two things to be said. Passive suffering is a theme inappropriate to great literature only if it is considered meaningful in and of itself, and unrelated to larger meanings. It is precisely Owen's capacity for relating passive suffering, "the pity war distilled," to such meanings that enables him to control his material and his emotions and to attain his "detachment" and "distance from the personal and the ordinary." His ability to place personal suffering within a far larger context of meaning and of value is what gives his great poems their enduring and timeless quality. It is hard that a poet should be condemned on the one hand for overemphasis on physical details and personal emotions and on the other for "almost God-like" detachment. In fact, one of Owen's great achievements is his wedding of the world of the flesh to that of the imagination and the spirit.

Those who speak of "passivity" appear to think of action exclusively in physical terms. Owen's poetry at its best is positive and affirmative, not merely negative. Its action is that of mind and spirit, not bodily action. And in this emphasis it is true to the realities with which it deals. For one of the central realities of modern life as of modern war is the increasing helplessness of the individual to take meaningful action. In peace or war he is pitted against inhuman and mechanical powers with which he cannot successfully contend. He can, if he has the virtue and the courage, keep his mind clear and his spirit unfettered by allegiance to hypocrisy, cruelty, and pride. He can maintain his inner integrity. This Owen did, in his life and in his poetry. It is doubtful whether any man of his generation or ours can do more.

II *Poetry and Propaganda*

Was Owen, by insisting on the poet's duty to warn, oversimplifying the meaning and function of poetry? This question poses the old quarrel between those who believe in "art for art's sake" and those who believe that art must serve social ends. It is a quarrel only because conceptions both of art and of social function are too often narrow and limited or warped from their true meaning.

If "society" means a collocation of institutions and attitudes that encourage and enable people to live as human beings, and "social function" means humanizing and serving them, Keats's "Ode on a Grecian Urn," that great work of art, cannot be considered of less real utility than Edwin Markham's "The Man with the Hoe," or— a more extreme example—Sarah Cleghorn's "The Golf Links Lie So Near the Mill." Surely it may rather be argued that great art must of necessity serve social ends, since art expresses and embodies a vision of truth, and as was said long ago, "Ye shall know the truth, and the truth shall make you free." It is only when the broader vision of art clashes with the limited and particular views and goals of a given society that the two are seemingly at odds. Society in the larger sense, art must always serve.

Art itself, of course, is sometimes untrue to its nature, gazing into a mirror at its own countenance or occupying itself with the peripheral and the merely decorative rather than the essential. Most of Owen's early verse is "arty" in this way. His later poems, if there were no other evidence, would alone demonstrate that there is no necessary conflict between art and social function, "propaganda," if that dishonored word may still be understood in a general and denotative sense. When Wilfred Owen turned from his juvenile conception of poetry to propaganda, from beauty to truth, he created true works of art, more real and more enduring than the feverish and flimsy poetic dreams of his early youth. For Keats was right, "Beauty is truth, truth beauty"; but it is only by the power of art that they can be perceived as one.

III *The "Key" to Owen's Poetry*

The critical questions just discussed have at least the merit of being issues posed by the nature of Owen's poetry, its subject matter and its attitudes, or by theories concerning the nature and function of art itself. It is right and proper that such questions should be debated, and different temperaments will perhaps always return different answers to them. But of late a charge has been made that the "key" to Owen's poetry must be sought and may be found in the circumstances of his life, the nature of his personality, and the emotional motivations that may be identified behind the themes and attitudes of his poems. According to Professor Joseph Cohen of Newcomb College, this key is the revelation that Wilfred Owen was a latent homosexual—a revelation vouchsafed to Cohen by the detailed portrait of Wilfred as he was in early youth amid his family in Harold Owen's memoirs, *Journey from Obscurity*.[12]

Concerning the charge itself, nothing need be said save that it is equally impossible either to prove or to disprove. Conclusive evidence of homosexuality that is not overt but remains latent can be obtained only in psychiatric treatment of a patient. But it is not possible to psychoanalyze a dead man. The behavior which

Cohen adduces may to him be suggestive, but it is not and cannot be evidence.

Of far more moment for critics and readers of poetry, however, is the question whether homosexuality, even if granted, can be considered the "key" to an understanding of Owen's poetry or that of any other poet; whether, in fact, emotional motivations, whatever they may be suspected to have been, are relevant to a consideration of a poet's achievement. Homosexuality does not in itself write any poem; and, once written, poems must be judged by criteria other than their supposed exhibition of homosexual motivations. Even if it could be proved that Wilfred Owen was indeed a latent homosexual, what of significance does this tell us about his poetry? Not much. Those who care for poetry will wish to look at poems rather than play a game admittedly fascinating but dangerous to good criticism and destructive to good poetry.

The dangers of reading poetry in the flickering light of special pleading are clearly revealed in Cohen's treatment of the poems themselves. Concentration on what he believes to be his discovery of Owen's latent homosexuality leads Cohen to make statements about individual poems that are dubious indeed. These range from the misinterpretation of a line to comments that distort the impact of a whole poem. "Some say God caught them even before they fell," from "Spring Offensive" poses, Cohen asserts, "the question whether the gesture is one of tender recovery or of compelling blood-lust." [13] The line in question, in the context in which it occurs, will not bear this interpretation.

Much less convincing is Cohen's sweeping statement that "all of his best known trench poems can be legitimately read as studies in injustice-collecting." [14] ("Injustice-collecting" is the homosexual's habit of seeking satisfaction in defeat, humiliation, privation, and depression, a habit Cohen believes is demonstrated in Wilfred's behavior in the family circle.) To say, as Cohen does, that "Strange Meeting" "laments the unjust deprivation of future fulfillment" [15] is to distort that great vision out of all recognition. To call the magnificent last stanza of "Insensibility" a study in injustice-collecting is to demonstrate the insensibility which the poem, in Cohen's phrase, "rails against." "Anthem for Doomed Youth" is not, as Cohen claims, a record of the "injustice of battle-zone burial." [16] "The Show" is a vision of the bestiality and universal guilt of war; to say that it "expounds victimization on several levels" [17] does not seem either an accurate or an adequate description of its meaning. And the depiction of the battle-front as a dead male body—"no insistence on Mother Earth here," [18] says Cohen— would seem to require no more esoteric explanation than that soldiers are customarily male. Bayonets and cartridges may indeed be obvious phallic symbols, but (we are reminded of the famous story of Freud and his cigar) they are also real weapons and inflict real wounds.

More doubtful still are Cohen's interpretations of Owen's general themes and attitudes as evidence of homosexual proclivities. If attachment to the figure of Christ and invocation of Him as a symbol of self-sacrificing love is enough to label a man a latent homosexual, what poet in the Western tradition could escape? More specifically, the poets of World War I, good and bad, appealed to the compassion of Jesus again and again, and analogized the suffering of soldiers to His in poem after poem. Sassoon's "The Redeemer" is only one of many instances. The difference lies in the subtlety and power with which Owen used Jesus as a symbol. The same comment applies to his treatment of women and of authority-figures like fathers, generals, or God. Similar attitudes were felt and expressed by his fellow poets and, in a different way, by common soldiers. Here again, Sassoon's "Base Details," "The General," and "Glory of Women" are particular instances of very widespread feelings.

Owen's theme of guilt may, as Cohen claims, reflect his feelings of estrangement from his father, and his emphasis on sacrifice, on the soldier's "greater love," may indeed "bespeak the essence of idealistic homosexuality";[19] but, if so, Owen shares that infirmity not only with poets, philosophers, and theologians for these two thousand years and more but with ordinary men and women of all times and places. The great basic emotions of anger, pity, love, and guilt are common to all humanity. Indeed, we are all bisexual. There is a sense in which it may be argued that all art, all civilization, is a sublimation of sexual feelings; and—according to Freud —sex enters into and affects all our relationships and actions, as it shapes our personalities.

There is, of course, nothing new or startling in the recognition of erotic motifs and emotions in modern war literature. A recent article by Richard Fein, "Modern War Poetry," discusses at some length the overwhelming prominence of sexual themes and images in the war poetry of this century.[20] Sexual feeling and the sexual act are the only normal peacetime experiences intense enough to bear comparison with the emotions and actions of battle. Moreover, images which recall the vital assertion of one's being oppose, control, and deny the otherwise intolerable fear of destruction. Love and death are the twin poles of human experience, and in the sex act they are in a sense combined: it is no accident that the French call sexual climax "the little death." So the intense emotions of battle may be felt and expressed in terms of sexual experience. So many poets have expressed them; a fact which renders unnecessary any special reading of Owen's war poems.

IV Owen's Contemporaries

In the perspective of nearly fifty years, what may be said of Wilfred Owen's achievement by comparison with that of his fellow war poets, particularly the best known of them or those who had at that time the greatest reputation: Rupert Brooke, Edward Thomas, Siegfried Sassoon, Edmund Blunden, Robert Graves, Robert Nichols, and Isaac Rosenberg? These men, except for the somewhat older Thomas, were his contemporaries. All of them, save for Brooke, like him were acquainted with the trench warfare of the Western Front; and their verse, like his, was conditioned by the circumstances of that war. Brooke died early in 1915, having taken part in but one engagement; Thomas was killed at Arras in 1917; and Rosenberg, a year later. Nichols saw only a few weeks of active service, being invalided out after the Battle of the Somme with shell shock from which he never wholly recovered. Sassoon, Blunden, and Graves all saw extensive service and survived the war. Sassoon died early in 1968; Blunden and Graves are still living.

Of them all, Brooke is still most readily associated with the poetry of World War I, particularly by people who read little poetry, and for reasons that have little to do with the actual verse Brooke wrote. Rupert Brooke is a demonstration of the otherwise dubious truth of the saying that whom the gods love die young. He was already at the time of his death the best known of the younger Georgian poets, those whose verse appeared in Edward Marsh's several anthologies, *Georgian Poetry*, beginning in 1912. His popularity was in large part due to his friendship with Marsh, whose enthusiasm for the man and the poet led him to champion Brooke's poetry (Brooke's *Poems* had been published in 1911) and to introduce the young man to a wide and important literary circle. It is perhaps difficult now to realize that it required some courage for Marsh to act as Brooke's literary mentor. Poems like "Channel Passage" and "Menelaus and Helen" were capable of shocking readers at that time by their daring realism and cynicism, and Brooke's arrogance and deliberate flouting of long-cherished poetic conventions annoyed many of his contemporaries.

On the outbreak of World War I, after his first reaction of shock, confusion, and grief for the friends he had so lately known in Germany, Brooke joined the Royal Naval Division and died only a few months later of blood poisoning on the island of Scyros in the Aegean, en route to Gallipoli. His death began a kind of apotheosis. Dean Inge quoted his sonnet "If I should die, think only this of me" from the pulpit of St. Paul's; Winston Churchill's letter to *The Times* expressed the nation's sense of loss; and Brooke's friends hastened to pour out poetic tributes to him. In the mind of the general public he still remains the archetype of brave and sacrificial youth, of the soldier-poet who gave both his life and his poetry for his country's cause.

Despite its technical accomplishment, however, Brooke's verse —and perhaps particularly the group of sonnets which are his war poems—has not worn very well. The differences between the war poems of Brooke and those of Owen lie in the very different attitudes of the two men toward themselves as poets and toward the subject of their verse. "Wilfred Owen," remarks a recent critic, "is the war poet for those who desire the reality, by contrast with Brooke, who is for those who are fascinated by the 'idea' of poetry." [21] This harsh comment, but a true one, goes far to explain why Brooke's poetry has had more popular appeal than Owen's. As Eliot's bird tells us, "Mankind cannot bear very much reality." The same judgment is echoed in more specific terms by another commentator on the two poets: "Brooke saw himself and was seen by others as the conscious trustee of England's values. Owen, on the contrary, depersonalized himself, made himself transparent to the sufferings of others, so as to transmit these as they really were." [22]

Brooke's war sonnets suffer from shallowness of feeling and

from what seems like refusal to face realities or actual inability to grasp them. Skillful as they are, they are hollow at the core; their rhetoric awakens only its own echoes, not the affirmation of either mind or heart. They are marred by self-consciousness and self-dramatization. It would be unfair to say that they are consciously dishonest, but they certainly exhibit none of the unrelenting honesty of observation and the acceptance of reality that mark Owen's poems. These poems also lie open to Johnston's charge that the war poets express emotions purely personal, and their power is further limited by the fact that the emotions they express seem to a later generation so conventional as to be unconvincing and unreal. No doubt patriotism is as valid an emotion as pity; but, like pity, "it must be generated and objectified within a large tragic context" if it is to support a tragic vision. Brooke's war sonnets, whatever may be the truth about the honesty and value of the feelings behind them, do not succeed in objectifying these feelings in a manner which still has meaning. And their inadequacies grow more and more obvious as time passes in contrast with Owen's impersonality and selflessness, his realism, his emotional and moral power.

After Brooke's death, Robert Nichols was for a time the most popular of the war poets. In Sassoon's autobiography *Siegfried's Journey* he tells how Nichols's *Ardours and Endurances,* published in the same month as Sassoon's own volume of poems, *The Old Huntsman,* had made Nichols the most successful soldier-poet of the year: "In fact his sales had much exceeded mine." [23] Nichols became greatly in demand for readings of his poetry in London literary circles, and his appearances in turn helped to spread knowledge of him and his verse.

According to Sassoon, Owen thought Nichols "self-concerned and vaniteux in his verse." [24] A poem like "Thanksgiving" illustrates the qualities of which Owen complains. Nichols's poetry, further, is artificial in its expression of feeling—however sincere the feelings themselves may have been—and derivative in form. He clearly shows the influence of poets as dissimilar as A. E. Housman and Walt Whitman; but it is Housman's tricks of manner that Nichols imitates, not his poignant and lyric lamentation; and Whitman's worst qualities appear in "Casualty" without a trace of Whitman's genius. "Casualty," indeed, in its forced and rhetorical emotion that becomes bathos, as well as in its diction, reads al-

most like a parody of Whitman. It is a commentary on poetic popularity that verse of this caliber should have been more palatable
to the London public than Sassoon's genuine if limited poetry. But
time has taken its revenge, and Nichols's verse is no longer important save perhaps to the literary historian of the period.

With Sassoon the case is very different. He had genuine gifts as
a satirist, and his satirical verse still has force and carries conviction. His emotions of anger and contempt were both real and relevant, and he found expression for them in swift, pungent, colloquial verse, realistic in diction if traditional in form. Nor did he
lack feelings more sensitive and profound than those expressed in
such satiric verses as "Base Details," "Blighters," "Suicide in the
Trenches," or "The General." Sassoon's "The Redeemer" employs
Owen's own analogy of the soldier to Christ; "A Working Party"
and "The Death Bed" show that Owen had no monopoly on the
theme of pity; "Concert Party" is a study in the nostalgia and
homesickness that are inseparable from the soldier's experience of
war; and "Aftermath" combines realism with a poignant anguish
that still shakes the heart.

However, Sassoon lacks Owen's art, his moral fervor, and the
scope and range of his vision. His verse is true, but its truth is
particular rather than universal. He is poet but not prophet: he
sees men in the context of their immediate situation, not in that of
history or of eternity. Despite his sensitivity, he has none of
Owen's spiritual quality nor his basically religious outlook. And he
has little of Owen's concern with the shape and sound of words,
with cadence and rhythm. For all these reasons, Sassoon's verse
lacks the verbal interest, the intensity and depth, the perspective
of Owen's, and perhaps above all the splendor to which Owen
now and then attains of memorable and magnificent lines.

Robert Graves, who saw more active service than any other of
the war poets, can be as realistic as either Sassoon or Owen; but
his distinguishing characteristic is a lighthearted fancy, sometimes
macabre, sometimes merely playful. Humor is a quality conspicu-
ously absent from Owen's war poetry, and Sassoon's laughter has
a bitter and savage bite foreign to Graves's less sensitive and more
volatile temperament. Curiously enough, Graves's humor, flippant
as it sometimes is, links him instead with Isaac Rosenberg, a poet
otherwise wholly different, in such a poem as "The Immortals."
Rosenberg also exhibits a capacity for macabre fancy, though he

has nothing of Graves's gaiety. But humor of any sort is rare in the poetry of World War I; it was, as Graves has observed in one of his poems, "a queer time," certainly not a gay one. When Graves is serious he can be direct and moving, as in "The Last Post," or "Two Fusiliers"; but his verse has none of the depth, intensity, or vision of Owen's. It is difficult, in fact, to think of him as a war poet in the same sense as Owen, Sassoon, and Rosenberg. Graves has had a long and various literary career; and, though the war profoundly affected him, as it did all those who took part in it, it did not afterward furnish him either with subjects or attitudes.

Edmund Blunden, like Graves, served throughout almost the entire war, survived it, and has since had a distinguished career as poet, professor, and critic. Born in 1896, he was the youngest of all the war poets, a fact which could not be guessed from his verse. For so young a man, scarcely more than a boy, to have written such poems as "Thiepval Wood," "The Zonnebeke Road," "Festubert: the Old German line," and "Les Halles d'Ypres" is an achievement in itself. There is nothing in the least juvenile about them, in expression or in feeling. Their realism is as honest and as closely observed as anything in Owen. In fact, Blunden's word pictures of the devastation and desolation of the Western Front are unsurpassed in the poetry of the war. His verse is filled with the love of nature, and a sense of natural beauties and harmonies broken by war; in his prose memoir, *Undertones of War,* written some years afterward, he describes himself as "a harmless young shepherd in a soldier's coat." He too knew love and pity for his men and their sufferings, and he is never merely an observer but reflects and meditates upon the meaning of what he has experienced. Blunden is surely one of the best poets of the war. Yet as surely Owen surpasses him by the same qualities that raise his poetry above Sassoon's: by imagination, by scale of vision, by profundity of feeling and the linking of particular feelings and facts to the ultimate realities of man's nature and fate.

Of all the war poets, Isaac Rosenberg comes closest to Owen in those qualities in which Owen surpasses the others, but the effect of Rosenberg's verse is quite different. Feeling in his poems becomes passionate in its life, always in the active voice, struggling to release itself from the bondage of words. And the words struggle to contain and to express it. Rosenberg's verse is full of tension and violence, the poet's vivid imagination and fervent feeling wrestling with his medium, in his best poems triumphing, though hardly. He knows the extremes of terror and of joy; he penetrates with awful clarity into pain and fear, wounds, death and corruption, and into love and beauty too. "Dead Man's Dump" is a vision of war, of bestiality, of waste and the perversion of man's nature and particularly of the ineluctable mystery of death as apocalyptic in its different way as Owen's "The Show." Rosenberg's descriptive passages are vividly concrete and at the same time unforgettable in their power of suggestion, and he has Owen's gift for memorable phrasing. The lines on the dead bodies in Rosenberg's "Dead Man's Dump" illustrate both qualities:

> Burnt black by strange decay
> Their sinister faces lie,
> The lid over each eye,
> The grass and coloured clay
> More motion have than they,
> Joined to the great sunk silences.

The final line of this passage is one of the most profoundly haunting and evocative to come out of the war.

But Rosenberg did not very often achieve such successes as "Dead Man's Dump," "Break of Day in the Trenches," or "Returning, We Hear the Larks." He remains greater in promise and potential than in actual performance, and he has left far fewer fine and finished poems than has Owen. His vision has the same sweep and scope; his imagination, if anything, is more vivid; his emotion more intense, though not more profound; and he has Owen's feeling for words and their sounds and rhythms. His was a great talent and his death a great loss to poetry; but his actual achievement does not equal that of Owen.

Edward Thomas was already thirty-six when the war began, the oldest by several years of this group of poets, and a professional writer since his undergraduate days. He had but lately turned from criticism to poetry, under the influence of Robert Frost, then a resident in England. In his love of nature, of the rhythms of country life and the small, ordinary things of the countryside, he may be compared with Frost; but his verse has its own very different and individual idiom and a tone quieter, sadder, more resigned than Frost's. Thomas's poetry combines sharp observation with delicate sensitivity to things seen "not with but through the eye." His love of beauty is filled with pain at beauty's passing, and his tenderness embraces all living things because they live so short a time.

The verse Thomas wrote after the outbreak of war until his death in 1917 is very little if at all different from the verse he had written before. Unlike Owen, he did not find the war an experience that sundered him from earlier ways of feeling, thinking, and writing. War enters his verse as a background, adding poignancy to the beauty of nature and the brevity of life, but never becoming a subject in itself. Unlike the other war poets, he was not moved to anger or to protest in his verse, nor did his observation turn to descriptions of the horror of the trenches. "As the Team's Head-Brass" is a picture of war's impact on the lives of English countrymen at home in England, its pity and pain and loss accepted quietly as part of the life of man in a universe mysterious to men. "A Private" is reminiscent of Hardy's "Drummer Hodge" in its recollection of a ploughman dead in battle.

Thomas is a poet and a good one, who might have written something great. No more than Owen did he belong among the Georgian poets. His is true poetry: true to fact and to feeling, true to life, true in diction, with nothing artificial, derivative, or mannered about it. Save for Owen, he is perhaps the most gifted of this group. Of him it is easier to predict than of Owen and Rosenberg what the future might have held, for his talent was already developed and his poetic line clear. But he is not in any meaningful sense a war poet.

V   *Final Verdict*

It has become clearer and clearer in the years since Owen's death that both in talent and in achievement he was the greatest of the poets who wrote during and of World War I. Many of the poems he had time to write are, by any criterion, great; what he might have achieved, given more time, is impossible to predict—and also irrelevant in making a final judgment. Would he, as the poets of the 1930's declared, have found in social injustice a subject like war that would have stirred his imagination and his emotions sufficiently to produce great poetry? Or, as Day Lewis suggests, might "his honesty, fervour and sensuousness . . . have been directed elsewhere to produce a Catullan kind of love-poetry"? [25] It does not seem likely that he would have found himself written out, or been forced to turn back continually to his war experiences for inspiration. He had prepared himself as a poet from boyhood; he had met the challenge of war with magnificent poetic strength, creating poems so different from his earlier verse as to seem written by a different man; his mind, heart, and talent were still developing and maturing. But for him there was no more time, and what might have been we cannot know for sure. "The loss of Owen, Thomas, and Rosenberg was more damaging to the future of English poetry than the loss, bad as it was, of the more conventional Brooke," [26] says R. C. Churchill in his chapter on "The Age of T. S. Eliot" in the *Concise History of English Literature;* and with this verdict most critics in the 1960's would agree.

If what Owen might have done cannot be known, we know what he did. Failing in his purpose of warning, he yet wrote poems which remain a living and a growing influence upon the minds of those who read them. His experiments in assonance and half-rhyme were soon assimilated and have long been used as a matter of course by contemporary poets. His diction played a part in revitalizing and refreshing the vocabulary of poetry and his experiments, together with those of Gerard Manley Hopkins, doubtless encouraged the free and uninhibited playing with language and syntax that has been a prominent feature of modern verse. F. W. Bateson has pronounced Owen "the one modern poet whom it is impossible not to hear," and compared his poetry in "its vigour, its freshness, and its tenacity, with that of such a forerunner of Augustan poetry as Rochester," though he warns also that it is too soon to be certain if the main body of modern poetry will follow in the same direction.[27]

It is possible to see Owen's poetry, as has one critic at least, as "the strongest link between the poetry of the nineteenth century and that of today," [28] both for its technical interest and for Owen's effort to comprehend war and its significance to the age in which he lived, and in which we too must live: "It is now clear that Owen was the outstanding English poet of the First World War, and, because the Second World War was a continuation of it, of that too. War has been the central horror of European history in this century; and Owen, mourning young lives tormented and treated as expendable, was to speak as directly to mourners in 1945 as to those of 1918; furthermore, since the fear of war is now

universal, his elegies speak to us directly. They are a warning." [29]
So writes William Plomer in his Preface to Benjamin Britten's
War Requiem. And so different a voice as Dylan Thomas's repeats
his verdict. Thomas's poetry, unlike Owen's as it is, still bears
marks of his influence: see "The Force that Through the Green
Fuse Drives the Flower," for example, for a sophisticated use of
assonance and half-rhyme. He names Owen as one of the four
most profound influences upon the poets who came after him—
the other three being Hopkins, the later Yeats, and Eliot—and
declares, like Plomer, that "now the poetry of Wilfred Owen
speaks to us . . . with terrible new significance and strength.
. . . [We] can see, re-reading Owen, that he is a poet of all times,
all places, and all wars." [30]

This last point, perhaps, most needs to be emphasized in any
final appraisal of Wilfred Owen's achievement. His subject was
war; but, as Richard Fein reminds us, "All the good war poetry of
this century has a double focus, disastrous reality and that dimension in which war magnifies and dramatizes the fundamental
forms of our experience. . . . War poetry declares and explores
the conditions of our general existence. War is the backdrop
against which the overall reality of human experience can be discovered." [31]

Owen's poetry, in a greater degree than that of any of his contemporaries, demonstrates the truth of this statement. Setting out
to tell the truth about war, he succeeded in telling what he perceived and felt to be the truth of human existence. It may be that
neither poets nor statesmen can save humanity from the agony of
war. But out of that agony Wilfred Owen created poems that live
and speak to all who will hear. And his poems remain, in Dylan
Thomas's words, "their anguish unabated, their beauty for ever,
their truth manifest, their warning unheeded." [32]

Notes and References

Chapter One

1. Harold Owen, *Journey from Obscurity, Wilfred Owen 1893–1918: Memoirs of the Owen Family* (London, 1963), I, 1. Details concerning Wilfred Owen's early years, family life, and personality are based for the most part on these memoirs of the Owen family, but all inferences or opinions expressed are my own.

2. Edmund Blunden, "Memoir" (1931), in *The Collected Poems of Wilfred Owen*, ed. C. Day Lewis (London, 1963), p. 148. All references to Blunden's "Memoir" or to C. Day Lewis' "Introduction" and all quotations from Wilfred Owen's poems are taken from this volume.

3. Harold Owen, I, 103.

4. *Ibid.*, p. 131.

5. *Ibid.*, p. 122.

6. *Ibid.*, p. 149.

7. *Ibid.*, p. 253.

8. *Ibid.*, II, 202.

9. C. Day Lewis, "Introduction," *The Collected Poems of Wilfred Owen*, p. 17.

10. Harold Owen, *Journey from Obscurity*, III, 121.

11. Blunden, "Memoir," p. 160.

12. *Ibid.*, p. 162.

13. Harold Owen, *Journey from Obscurity*, III, 155.

14. *Ibid.*, 155.

15. Blunden, "Memoir," p. 164.

16. *Ibid.*, p. 164.

17. *Ibid.*, p. 165.

18. Sassoon had written anonymously and printed privately several volumes of verse prior to *The Old Huntsman*. The latter, however, was the first publication to bear his name, and it is most unlikely that Owen had read the earlier books or would have known they were by Sassoon if he had.

19. Siegfried Sassoon, *Siegfried's Journey 1916–1920* (New York, 1946), p. 106.

20. Blunden, "Memoir," p. 172.

21. *Ibid.*, p. 173.

22. *Ibid.*, p. 171.

23. Harold Owen, *Journey from Obscurity*, III, 123.

24. C. Day Lewis, "Introduction," p. 31.

25. From MS. 43720, British Museum.

26. Blunden, "Memoir," p. 170.

27. *Ibid.*, p. 167.

28. C. Day Lewis, "Introduction," p. 23.

29. Blunden, "Memoir," p. 178.

30. D. S. R. Welland, *Wilfred Owen: A Critical Study* (London, 1960), p. 68.

31. C. Day Lewis, ed., *The Collected Poems of Wilfred Owen* (London, 1964), p. 89n.

32. That Mrs. Owen was personally responsible for the choice of this poem and for the change of punctuation is testified to by Harold Owen in a private letter to me.

Chapter Two

1. Walter Jackson Bate, *John Keats* (Cambridge, 1963), p. 140.

2. John Keats, "Sleep and Poetry," ll. 246–47.

3. John Keats, "Ode" [Bards of Passion and of Mirth].

4. William Wordsworth, "The Solitary Reaper."

5. "The One Remains."

6. "Happiness."

7. "The Sleeping Beauty."

8. C. Day Lewis, ed., *The Collected Poems of Wilfred Owen*, note on "Song of Songs," p. 126.

9. Algernon Charles Swinburne, "Dolores."

10. Swinburne, "Hymn to Proserpine."

11. Harold Owen, *Journey from Obscurity*, III, 163.

12. Loiseau, "A Reading of Wilfred Owen's Poems," *English Studies*, XXI (June, 1939), 108.

13. *Ibid.*, p. 106.

14. C. Day Lewis, ed., *The Collected Poems of Wilfred Owen*, note on "Maundy Thursday," p. 136.

Chapter Three

1. John Fletcher, "Wilfred Owen Re-edited," *Etudes Anglaises*, XVII (Avril–Juin, 1964), 177.

2. W. B. Yeats, ed., *The Oxford Book of Modern Verse* (New York, 1937), p. xxxiv.

3. This letter is quoted in Joseph Cohen's "Owen Agonistes," *English Literature in Transition 1880–1920*, VIII (December, 1965), 259.

4. Babette Deutsch, *Poetry in Our Time* (New York, 1963), p. 392.

5. Stephen Spender, "Poetry and Pity," in *The Destructive Element* (London, 1935), p. 218.

6. Ezekiel 37:3.

7. Revelations 21:1.

8. Luke 23:21–29.

9. D. S. R. Welland, *Wilfred Owen: A Critical Study* (London, 1960), p. 74.

10. For detailed discussions of "Strange Meeting," see Samuel J. Hazo, "The Passion of Wilfred Owen," *Renascence*, XI (Summer, 1959), 201–8, and Elliott B. Gose, Jr., "Digging In: An Interpretation of Wilfred Owen's 'Strange Meeting,' " *College English*, XXII (March, 1961), 417–19.

11. Dylan Thomas, "Wilfred Owen," in *Quite Early One Morning* (London, 1954), p. 92.

12. "Requiem for a Dead Soldier," *The Times Literary Supplement*, November 7, 1963, p. 903.

Chapter Four

1. C. Day Lewis, *The Collected Poems of Wilfred Owen*, p. 24.

2. D. S. R. Welland was the first to suggest the poetry of Jules Romains as a source for Wilfred Owen's half-rhyme in "Half-Rhyme in Wilfred Owen: Its Derivation and Use," *Review of English Studies*, n.s. I (July, 1950), 226–41. Later, in Chapter VI of his book *Wilfred Owen: A Critical Study*, he discussed the subject in greater detail. Examination of Romains' *Petit Traité de Versification* has convinced me that Dr. Welland's theory is right.

3. *Faber Book of Modern Verse*, ed. Michael Roberts (London, 1936), p. 28.

4. David I. Masson, "Wilfred Owen's Free Phonetic Patterns: Their Style and Function," *Journal of Aesthetics and Art Criticism*, XIII (March, 1955), 361. I am indebted to this excellent analysis of Owen's sound patterns for some of the material in this chapter.

Chapter Five

1. John Middleton Murry, "Present Condition of English Poetry," in *Aspects of Literature* (New York, 1920), pp. 145–47.

2. Solomon Eagle [Sir John C. Squire], "A New War Poet," *The Living Age*, CCCVIII (February 5, 1921), 370.

3. E[dmund] B[lunden], "The Real War," *The Athenaeum* (December 10, 1920), p. 807.

4. *The Spectator*, CXXV (December 18, 1920), 821.

5. Edmund Blunden, "The Real War," p. 807.

6. "Poetry," *The London Mercury*, III (1921), 334–35.

7. *The Times Literary Supplement*, December 16, 1920, p. 862.

8. H. P. Collins, *Modern Poetry* (London, 1925), p. 60.

9. Ifan Kyrle Fletcher, "The Poetry of Wilfred Owen," *Welsh Outlook*, XV (November, 1928), 332–33.

10. Henry Williamson, "Reality in War Literature," *The London Mercury*, XIX (January, 1929), 299.

11. Siegfried Sassoon, "Wilfred Owen—A Personal Appreciation," in *A Tribute to Wilfred Owen*, compiled by T. J. Walsh (Birkenhead: Birkenhead Institute, 1964), p. 40.

12. Alan Porter, "Reviews of New Books," *Voices*, V (January, 1931), 93.

13. *Ibid.*, 93.

14. *Ibid.*, 93.

15. Stanley J. Kunitz, "Poet of the War," *Poetry*, XL (June, 1932), 162.

16. Alan Porter, *op. cit.*, p. 93.

17. Stanley J. Kunitz, *op. cit.*, p. 162.

18. *The Spectator*, CXLVI (June 6, 1931), 905.

19. Inconstant Reader, "Preferences," *Canadian Forum*, XII (November, 1931), 58–60.

20. Richard Church, untitled review, *New Statesman and Nation*, I (April 11, 1931), 256.

21. Theodore Morrison, "Bookshelf," *The Atlantic Monthly*, CXLIX (January, 1932), 14.

22. Horace Gregory, "A Dead Poetic Movement," *The Nation*, CXXXIII (November 25, 1931), 577.

23. I. M. Parsons, "The Poems of Wilfred Owen (1893–1918)," *The Criterion*, X (July, 1931), 667.

24. *Ibid.*, pp. 666–67.

25. "Wilfred Owen, 1893–1918," in *Authors Today and Yesterday*, ed. Stanley J. Kunitz (New York, 1933), p. 511.

26. C. Day Lewis, *A Hope for Poetry* (Oxford, 1934), p. 17.

27. C. Day Lewis, *The Buried Day* (London, 1960), p. 217.

28. C. Day Lewis, *The Collected Poems of Wilfred Owen*, p. 12.

29. Stephen Spender, "Poetry and Pity," pp. 219–21.

30. Stephen Spender, *World Within World* (New York, 1951), p. 128.

31. Christopher Isherwood, *Lions and Shadows* (New York, 1947), pp. 179–80.

32. James G. Southworth, "Stephen Spender," in *Sowing the Spring* (Oxford, 1940), p. 153.

33. Stephen Spender, *World Within World*, p. 86.

34. John Bayley, "But for Beaumont-Hamel," *The Spectator*, CCXI (October 4, 1963), 419.

35. Louis MacNeice, "Out of Ugliness," *New Statesman*, LX (1960), 624.

36. Monroe K. Spears, *The Poetry of W. H. Auden* (New York, 1963), p. 21.

37. David Daiches, "The Poetry of Wilfred Owen," in *New Literary Values: Studies in Modern Literature* (Edinburgh, 1936) p. 64.

38. W. B. Yeats, ed., *The Oxford Book of Modern Verse* (New York, 1936), pp. xxxiv–xxxv.

39. *The Letters of W. B. Yeats*, ed. Allen Wade (London, 1954), p. 874.

40. Richard Ellmann, *Yeats, the Man and the Masks* (New York, 1948), p. 290.

41. *Ibid.*, p. 214.

42. *Ibid.*, p. 201.

43. *Ibid.*, p. 205.

44. Curtis Bradford, *Yeats at Work* (Carbondale, Ill., 1965), pp. 16–17.

45. Richard Ellmann, *op. cit.*, p. 250.

46. *Ibid.*, p. 278.

47. W. B. Yeats, "The Song of the Happy Shepherd."

48. See D. S. Savage, "Two Prophetic Poems," *Western Review*, XIII (Winter, 1949), 67–78, for a very interesting discussion of these two poems, although his statements about Yeats's attitude seem extreme to me: "Each of these two poets, in his own way, penetrated to the heart of the human historical situation, and defined in himself, with admirable devotion and clarity, one of the only two thoroughly consistent and coherent attitudes towards that course. Yeats wrote in affirmation of the Beast, of blood and of war. . . . Owen positively renounced brutalization and blood."

49. See bibliography by William White, published by Kent State University Press, for a list of articles by these critics.

50. See bibliography below.

51. J. C. Maxwell, untitled review, *Notes and Queries*, n.s. IX (March, 1962), 119.

Chapter Six

1. G. S. Fraser, *The Modern Writer and His World* (Baltimore, 1964), p. 266.

2. John H. Johnston, *English Poetry of the First World War* (Princeton, 1964), p. x.

3. *Ibid.*, pp. x–xi.

4. *Ibid.*, pp. 252–53.

5. *Ibid.*, p. 335.

6. *Ibid.*, p. 191.

7. *Ibid.*, pp. 205–6.

8. W. B. Yeats, ed., *The Oxford Book of Modern Verse*, p. xxxiv.

9. David Daiches, "The Poetry of Wilfred Owen," in *New Literary Values: Studies in Modern Literature* (Edinburgh, 1936), pp. 54–55.

10. Philip Larkin, "The War Poet," *The Listener*, LII (October 10, 1963), 561.

11. Unsigned review, "Requiem for a Dead Soldier," *The Times Literary Supplement*, November 7, 1963, p. 903.

12. Joseph Cohen, "Owen Agonistes," *English Literature in Transition (1880–1920)*, VIII (December, 1965), 254.

13. *Ibid.*, p. 260.

14. *Ibid.*, p. 262.

15. *Ibid.*, p. 262.

16. *Ibid.*, p. 262.

17. *Ibid.*, p. 262.

18. *Ibid.*, p. 262.

19. *Ibid.*, p. 265.

20. Richard Fein, "Modern War Poetry," *Southwest Review*, XLVII (Autumn, 1962), 279–88.

21. D. J. Enright, "The Literature of the First World War," in *The Modern Age*, ed. Boris Ford, Vol. VII of *Pelican Guide to English Literature* (Baltimore, 1961), 161.

22. Geoffrey Matthews, "Brooke and Owen," *Stand*, IV (No. 3, 1964), 33–34.

23. Siegfried Sassoon, *Siegfried's Journey 1916–1920*, p. 100.

24. *Ibid.*, p. 99.

25. C. Day Lewis, "Introduction," p. 24.

26. R. C. Churchill, "The Age of T. S. Eliot," in *The Concise Cambridge History of English Literature*, ed. George Sampson (2nd ed.; Cambridge, 1961), p. 960.

27. F. W. Bateson, *English Poetry and the English Language* (New York, 1961), pp. 121–22.

28. Howard Sergeant, "The Importance of Wilfred Owen," *English*, X (No. 55, 1954), 10.

29. William Plomer, "Preface" to Benjamin Britten, *War Requiem* (London: The Decca Record Co., Ltd.), p. [5].

30. Dylan Thomas, *Quite Early One Morning*, p. 92.

31. Richard Fein, "Modern War Poetry," p. 288.

32. Dylan Thomas, *op. cit.*, p. 92.

Selected Bibliography

The following is a highly selective bibliography of those studies I consider of most use in understanding and interpreting Owen. Much of the material on him consists of reviews and brief notices of no particular value, and I have made no attempt to list these. The reader is referred to the bibliography published by the Kent State University Press, and listed below.

PRIMARY SOURCES

Poems. With an Introduction by Siegfried Sassoon. London: Chatto & Windus, 1920.

Poems. A new edition, including many pieces now first published and notices of his life and work, by Edmund Blunden. London: Chatto & Windus, 1931.

Thirteen Poems. With Drawings by Ben Shahn. Northampton, Mass.: Gehenna Press, 1956. Texts of the poems reprinted from *Poems,* 1931.

The Collected Poems of Wilfred Owen. Edited with an Introduction and Notes by C. Day Lewis, and with a Memoir by Edmund Blunden. London: Chatto & Windus, 1963.

Collected Letters of Wilfred Owen, edited by John Bell and Harold Owen. London: Oxford University Press, 1967.

SECONDARY SOURCES

1. Bibliography

WHITE, WILLIAM. *Wilfred Owen (1893–1918): A Bibliography.* Kent, Ohio: Kent State University Press, 1967. Reprinted, with additions, from *The Serif,* II (December, 1965), 5–16. The only Owen bibliography, though not complete, contains virtually all the easily available material by and about Owen.

2. Studies

BERGONZI, BERNARD. *Heroes' Twilight: A Study of the Literature of the Great War.* London: Constable & Co., Ltd., 1965. Thorough

and excellent study; includes a chapter comparing Wilfred Owen
and Isaac Rosenberg.

BLUNDEN, EDMUND. "Mainly Wilfred Owen." *War Poets, 1914–1918*.
London: Longmans, Green & Co., for the British Council and the
National Book League (Writers and Their Work, No. 100), 1958.
Brief but good analysis of Owen's themes and attitudes, and the
general qualities of his poetry.

CAZAMIAN, LOUIS. *Symbolisme et poésie: l'exemple anglais*. Paris: La
Presse française et étrangère; Oreste Zeluck, éditeur, 1947. Excellent analysis and commentary on "Anthem for Doomed Youth."

COHEN, JOSEPH. "The War Poet as Archetypal Spokesman," *Stand*
(Leeds), IV, 3 (1964), 23–27. A protest against the "canoniza-
tion" of the soldier-poets. Cohen argues that such men as Rupert
Brooke and Wilfred Owen have "been robbed of their essential
humanity in order to make them archetypal spokesmen."

————. "Wilfred Owen's Greater Love," *Tulane Studies in English*,
VI (1956), 105–17. Analysis of Owen's spiritual point of view
based on a definition of the phrase "greater love." Cohen has since
repudiated the view expressed in this article, but it remains far
more cogent and sound than that developed in "Owen Agonistes"
(see below).

————. "Owen Agonistes," *English Literature in Transition* (*1880–
1920*) VIII (December, 1965), 254. Cohen argues that the "key"
to Owen's poetry may be found in his alleged homosexual motivations.

DAICHES, DAVID. "The Poetry of Wilfred Owen." *New Literary Values:
Studies in Modern Literature*. Edinburgh: Oliver and Boyd, 1936.
Relatively early but still one of the best brief commentaries on
Owen's poetry.

FAIRCHILD, HOXIE NEALE. "Toward Hysteria." *Religious Trends in
English Poetry. 1880–1920*. Vol. V. New York: Columbia University Press, 1962. Discussion of the attitudes of the World War
I poets toward orthodox religious belief. Very good on Owen's
view of Christianity.

FEIN, RICHARD. "Modern War Poetry," *Southwest Review*, XLVII
(Autumn, 1962), 279–88. Not specifically on Owen, but an important article on the themes and attitudes of modern war poetry.

FREEMAN, ROSEMARY. "Parody as a Literary Form: George Herbert
and Wilfred Owen," *Essays in Criticism*, XIII (October, 1963),
307–22. Deals particularly with "Greater Love."

GOSE, ELLIOTT B., JR. "Digging In: An Interpretation of Wilfred
Owen's 'Strange Meeting,' " *College English*, XXII (March, 1961),
417–19. Interesting analysis of "Strange Meeting."

HAZO, SAMUEL J. "The Passion of Wilfred Owen," *Renascence*, XI (Summer, 1959), 201–8. Analysis chiefly of "Greater Love," "Anthem for Doomed Youth," and "Strange Meeting," which Hazo considers "thematically entire."

JOHNSTON, JOHN H. "Poetry and Pity: Wilfred Owen." *English Poetry of the First World War: A Study in the Evolution of Lyric and Narrative Form.* Princeton: Princeton University Press, 1964. Fullest, most thoughtful study yet published of the poets of World War I. Johnston feels that, because of their concentration on the personal and the subjective, and their use primarily of the lyric mode, most of these poets, including Owen, failed to exploit fully the tragic potentialities of their material.

LOISEAU, J. "A Reading of Wilfred Owen's Poems," *English Studies*, XXI (June, 1939), 97–108. Good discussion of the general qualities of Owen's poetry, though M. Loiseau's thesis that Owen's war poetry represents a "perversion of his art" seems to me wholly mistaken.

MASSON, DAVID I. "Wilfred Owen's Free Phonetic Patterns: Their Style and Function," *Journal of Aesthetics and Art Criticism* (March, 1955), pp. 360–69. An invaluable study of Owen's internal alliterative and assonant patterns.

MATTHEWS, GEOFFREY. "Brooke and Owen," *Stand*, IV 3 (1964), 28–34. Comparison of the two poets; concludes that Owen's compassion finally distinguishes his war poetry from Brooke's.

PARSONS, I. M. "The Poems of Wilfred Owen (1893–1918)," *New Criterion*, X (July, 1931), 658–69. Earliest lengthy study of the qualities of Owen's poetry; still one of the best.

————, editor. *Men Who March Away: Poems of the First World War.* London: Chatto & Windus, 1965. Not only does Owen have more poems, thirteen, in this anthology than any of the thirty-three writers, but he is prominently mentioned in the Introduction.

PINTO, V. DE SOLA. *Crisis in English Poetry, 1880–1940.* London: Hutchinson's University Library, 1951. Chapter VI, "Trench Poets," concludes that "Owen is the most remarkable of all the English poets of the First World War."

ROUTH, H. V. "Sassoon, Owen, Blunden." *English Literature and Ideas in the Twentieth Century.* London: Methuen & Co., Ltd., 1948. Routh feels that "these three represent a quite numerous group which expressed or tried to express something more than disillusionment." They introduced a touch of denationalized humanitarianism, then unusual, which has since become a trend of contemporary verse, and helped to make current the anti-God sentiment already suggested by Housman and Hardy.

SASSOON, SIEGFRIED. *Siegfried's Journey 1916–1920*. New York: The Viking Press, 1946. Contains excerpts of letters from Owen.

SAVAGE, D. S. "Two Prophetic Poems," *Western Review*, XIII (Winter, 1949), 67–78. A comparison of Yeats's "Second Coming" and Owen's "Strange Meeting."

SITWELL, OSBERT. "Wilfred Owen," *Atlantic*, CLXXXVI (August, 1950), 37–42. Personal reminiscence of Owen by a friend and fellow poet.

SPENDER, STEPHEN. "Poetry and Pity." *The Destructive Element*. Boston: Houghton Mifflin & Co., 1936. Spender feels that Owen's "pity" is an inadequate emotion in poetry, and that had he lived he would have been compelled to adopt some particular political philosophy as inspiration for his poems.

THOMAS, DYLAN. "Wilfred Owen." *Quite Early One Morning*. London: J. M. Dent & Sons, Ltd., 1954. New York: New Directions, 1954. An eloquent appreciation of Owen's war poetry. Thomas himself was influenced to some extent by Owen's use of assonance and half-rhyme.

WALSH, T. J. (comp.). *A Tribute to Wilfred Owen*. Birkenhead: Birkenhead Institute, 1964. "This magazine commemorates the opening of the Wilfred Owen Memorial Library and is a tribute from his friends to Wilfred Owen, the distinguished poet, who attended Birkenhead Institute from 1900–1907." The collection contains a number of personal reminiscences and brief tributes, and several short essays on Owen's poetry.

WELLAND, D. S. R. "Half-Rhyme in Wilfred Owen: Its Derivation and Use," *Review of English Studies*, n.s. I (July, 1950), 226–41. The first identification of Owen's source for half-rhyme in the poetry of Jules Romains.

———. *Wilfred Owen: A Critical Study*. London: Chatto & Windus, 1960. The first, and until the publication of the present study the only, monograph on Owen. Contains valuable scholarly information and some criticism, but suffers from a lack of sharp focusing and consecutive development of topics.

———. "Wilfred Owen's Manuscripts," *The Times Literary Supplement*, June 15, 1956, p. 368; June 22, p. 384. The material in this article was later developed and expanded into Welland's book.

Index